Childhood & Adolescent Disorders

The State of Mental Illness and Its Therapy

Adjustment Disorders

Anxiety Disorders

Cognitive Disorders

Childhood & Adolescent Disorders

Dissociative Disorders

Eating Disorders

Impulse-Control Disorders

Mental Disorders Due to a Medical Condition

Mood Disorders

Obsessive-Compulsive Disorder

Personality Disorders

Postpartum Disorders

Premenstrual Disorders

Psychosomatic Disorders

Schizophrenia

Sexual Disorders

Sleep Disorders

Substance-Related Disorders

The FDA & Psychiatric Drugs: How a Drug Is Approved

The State of Mental Illness and Its Therapy

Childhood & Adolescent Disorders

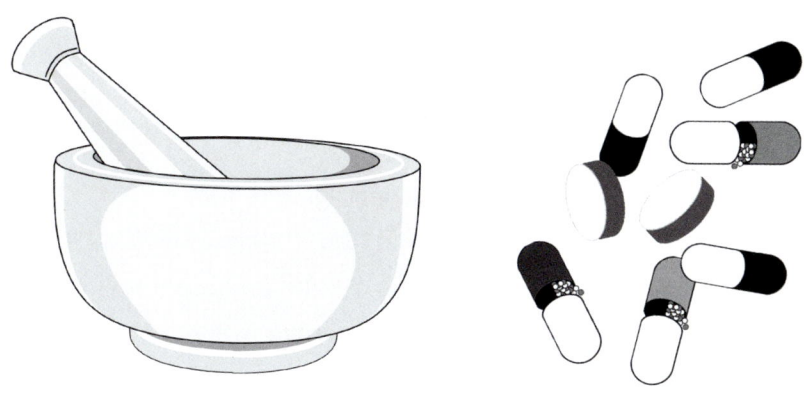

Shirley Brinkerhoff

Mason Crest
450 Parkway Drive, Suite D
Broomall, PA 19008
www.masoncrest.com

Copyright © 2014 by Mason Crest, an imprint of National Highlights, Inc. All rights reserved. No part of this publication may be reproduced or transmitted in any form or by any means, electronic or mechanical, including photocopying, recording, taping or any information storage and retrieval system, without permission from the publisher.

Printed in the Hashemite Kingdom of Jordan.

First printing
9 8 7 6 5 4 3 2 1

Series ISBN: 978-1-4222-2819-7
ISBN: 978-1-4222-2822-7
ebook ISBN: 978-1-4222-8983-9

The Library of Congress has cataloged the
   hardcopy format(s) as follows:

Library of Congress Cataloging-in-Publication Data

Brinkerhoff, Shirley.
  [Drug therapy and childhood and adolescent disorders]
  Childhood & adolescent disorders / Shirley Brinkerhoff.
     pages cm. – (The state of mental illness and its therapy)
  Audience: Age 12.
  Audience: Grade 7 to 8.
  Revision of: Drug therapy and childhood and adolescent disorders. 2004.
  Includes bibliographical references and index.
  ISBN 978-1-4222-2822-7 (hardcover) – ISBN 978-1-4222-2819-7 (series) – ISBN 978-1-4222-8983-9 (ebook)
  1. Pediatric psychopharmacology–Juvenile literature. 2. Child psychopathology–Juvenile literature. 3. Adolescent psychopathology–Juvenile literature. 4. Mentally ill children–Chemotherapy–Juvenile literature. 5. Psychotropic drugs–Juvenile literature. I. Title. II. Title: Childhood and adolescent disorders.
  RJ504.7.B75 2014
  616.89'180835–dc23
                         2013008192

Produced by Vestal Creative Services.
www.vestalcreative.com

This book is meant to educate and should not be used as an alternative to appropriate medical care. Its creators have made every effort to ensure that the information presented is accurate—but it is not intended to substitute for the help and services of trained professionals.

Picture credits:
18percentgrey | Dreamstime.com: p. 67. Anita Patterson Peppers | Dreamstime.com: p. 74. Artisticco Llc | Dreamstime.com: p. 102. Artville: pp. 101, 110, 112. Benjamin Stewart: pp. 53, 60, 63. Cheryl Casey | Dreamstime.com: p. 26. Comstock: pp. 12, 56, 73. Corbis: pp. 106, 113, 114. Corel: pp. 20, 23, 25, 29, 30, 31. Daniel Villeneuve | Dreamstime.com: p. 67. Dirk Ercken | Dreamstime.com: p. 19. Konstantin Sutyagin | Dreamstime.com: p. 68. Liz Van Steenburgh | Dreamstime.com: p. 10. Mauricio Jordan De Souza Coelho | Dreamstime.com: p. 105. Monkey Business Images | Dreamstime.com: p. 44. National Library of Medicine: pp. 46, 47, 50. Petar Neychev | Dreamstime.com: p. 95. Philippehalle | Dreamstime.com: p. 58. Photo Disc: pp. 72, 77, 86, 108. Photomax31 | Dreamstime.com: p. 98. Sabphoto | Dreamstime.com: p. 32. Stockbyte: pp. 70. Yuri Arcurs | Dreamstime.com: p. 14. The individuals in these images are models, and the images are for illustrative purposes only. The individuals in these images are models, and the images are for illustrative purposes only. To the best knowledge of the publisher, all other images are in the public domain. If any image has been inadvertently uncredited or miscredited, please notify Vestal Creative Services, Vestal, New York 13850, so that rectification can be made for future printings.

CONTENTS

Introduction 7

Foreword 9

1. Defining the Disorder 11

2. History of the Drugs 45

3. How Does the Drug Work? 57

4. Treatment Descriptions 73

5. Case Studies 87

6. Risks and Side Effects 99

7. Alternative and Supplementary Treatments 107

Further Reading 122

Film 123

For More Information 124

Index 126

About the Author & Consultants 128

Introduction
by Mary Ann McDonnell

Teenagers have reason to be interested in psychiatric disorders and their treatment. Friends, family members, and even teens themselves may experience one of these disorders. Using scenarios adolescents will understand, this series explains various psychiatric disorders and the drugs that treat them.

Diagnosis and treatment of psychiatric disorders in children between six and eighteen years old are well studied and documented in the scientific journals. A paper appearing in the *Journal of the American Academy of Child and Adolescent Psychiatry* in 2010 estimated that 49.5 percent of all adolescents aged 13 to 18 were affected by at least one psychiatric disorder. Various other studies have reported similar findings. Needless to say, many children and adolescents are suffering from psychiatric disorders and are in need of treatment.

Many children have more than one psychiatric disorder, which complicates their diagnoses and treatment plans. Psychiatric disorders often occur together. For instance, a person with a sleep disorder may also be depressed; a teenager with attention-deficit/hyperactivity disorder (ADHD) may also have a substance-use disorder. In psychiatry, we call this comorbidity. Much research addressing this issue has led to improved diagnosis and treatment.

The most common child and adolescent psychiatric disorders are anxiety disorders, depressive disorders, and ADHD. Sleep disorders, sexual disorders, eating disorders, substance-abuse disorders, and psychotic disorders are also quite common. This series has volumes that address each of these disorders.

Major depressive disorders have been the most commonly diagnosed mood disorders for children and adolescents. Researchers don't agree as to how common mania and bipolar disorder are in children. Some experts believe that manic episodes in children and adolescents are underdiagnosed. Many times, a mood disturbance may occur with another psychiatric disorder. For instance, children with ADHD may also be depressed. ADHD is just one psychiatric disorder that is a major health concern for children, adolescents, and adults. Studies of ADHD have reported prevalence rates among children that range from two to 12 percent.

Failure to understand or seek treatment for psychiatric disorders puts children and young adults at risk of developing substance-use disorders. For example, recent research indicates that those with ADHD who were treated with medication were 85 percent less likely to develop a substance-use disorder. Results like these emphasize the importance of timely diagnosis and treatment.

Early diagnosis and treatment may prevent these children from developing further psychological problems. Books like those in this series provide important information, a vital first step toward increased awareness of psychological disorders; knowledge and understanding can shed light on even the most difficult subject. These books should never, however, be viewed as a substitute for professional consultation. Psychiatric testing and an evaluation by a licensed professional is recommended to determine the needs of the child or adolescent and to establish an appropriate treatment plan.

Foreword
by Donald Esherick

We live in a society filled with technology—from computers surfing the Internet to automobiles operating on gas and batteries. In the midst of this advanced society, diseases, illnesses, and medical conditions are treated and often cured with the administration of drugs, many of which were unknown thirty years ago. In the United States, we are fortunate to have an agency, the Food and Drug Administration (FDA), which monitors the development of new drugs and then determines whether the new drugs are safe and effective for use in human beings.

When a new drug is developed, a pharmaceutical company usually intends that drug to treat a single disease or family of diseases. The FDA reviews the company's research to determine if the drug is safe for use in the population at large and if it effectively treats the targeted illnesses. When the FDA finds that the drug is safe and effective, it approves the drug for treating that specific disease or condition. This is called the labeled indication.

During the routine use of the drug, the pharmaceutical company and physicians often observe that a drug treats other medical conditions besides what is indicated in the labeling. While the labeling will not include the treatment of the particular condition, a physician can still prescribe the drug to a patient with this disease. This is known as an unlabeled or off-label indication. This series contains information about both the labeled and off-label indications of psychiatric drugs.

I have reviewed the books in this series from the perspective of the pharmaceutical industry and the FDA, specifically focusing on the labeled indications, uses, and known side effects of these drugs. Further information can be found on the FDA's website (www.FDA.gov).

Some psychiatric disorders are first diagnosed during adolescence.

Chapter One

Defining the Disorder

Some mental disorders are most often diagnosed in adulthood; others are not age specific and may show up at any time during an individual's life span. The disorders in this book, however, are most often diagnosed during childhood and adolescence.

This does not mean that there is always a clear boundary between childhood disorders and adult disorders. Although childhood and adolescent disorders begin in childhood, for various reasons they sometimes are not diagnosed until much later. Overall, however, these disorders usually present during the childhood and adolescent years, although they may last throughout an individual's entire life.

According to the *Diagnostic and Statistical Manual, fourth edition, text revision* (DSM-IV-TR), the most recent classification of mental disorders by the American Psychiatric Association), the following disorders are classified as usually first diagnosed in infancy, childhood, or adolescence:

- intellectual disabilities
- learning disorders
- pervasive developmental disorders
- attention-deficit and disruptive behavior disorders
- communication disorders
- motor skills disorders
- feeding and eating disorders of infancy or early childhood
- tic disorders
- elimination disorders
- other disorders of infancy, childhood, or adolescence

Psychiatric drugs are used to treat some of the disorders that are first diagnosed in childhood and adolescence.

Of these ten categories, only the four that are sometimes or often treated with psychiatric drugs will be dealt with in this book. These four are intellectual disabilities, pervasive developmental disorders, attention-deficit and disruptive behavior disorders, and tic disorders. The discovery and development of psychiatric drugs have moved forward rapidly in the last few decades, offering new help to many individuals who previously had little or no hope of finding help.

Tic Disorders

By the time Troy Sheridan was fifteen, he was so shy and withdrawn that he had almost no social life. He sat alone in the school lunchroom and walked to his classes by himself. After school he went to his room and stayed there, playing endless hours of Nintendo and listening to music.

But Troy hadn't always been a loner. Until the second grade, he'd been friendly and outgoing, a leader on the playground and a favorite among the kids who lived on his street.

Troy was seven when the problems began. His mother, Donna, could pinpoint the exact time his throat-clearing started, because it happened during the family's twelve-hour car trip to Cleveland to see Troy's grandparents. Troy cleared his throat off and on for the entire twelve hours.

"Troy, do you think you're getting a cold?" Donna asked during the first hour.

"Nope. I feel fine," he said, and turned another page in his Spiderman comic book.

"Well, then, would you like a drink?" she asked, handing him a juice box.

Troy shrugged. "Yeah, I guess so." He poked a plastic straw into the box and drained the juice in a few seconds.

But he began clearing his throat again almost immediately—once, then twice, then a dozen times. After a hundred more little coughs, and numerous requests to stop, his parents' nerves were frazzled.

"Troy, knock it off!" his fathered thundered, during hour ten of the trip. "I can't take this anymore."

"Sorry, Dad," Troy said. "I'm trying to stop. I just keep forgetting."

At Grandma's house, everyone had an opinion about Troy's "cough."

"Oh, just ignore it, Donna," Grandma told his mother and handed Troy a roll of cherry Lifesavers. "It'll go away."

"You better get him checked out for allergies. Or sinus troubles. I've always had trouble with my sinuses, you know." Grandpa put in.

When Troy's family got back to their hometown, Donna scheduled an appointment with the pediatrician. By now, Troy had developed a second habit: he kept blinking his eyes. Not the normal kind of blinking, but a tight, squinching together of his eyelids, sometimes twenty or thirty times per minute.

When his mother took him to the pediatrician, Troy showed no sign of either habit. Donna had assumed he would blink and cough

Tics may include facial grimaces or other unusual expressions.

throughout the appointment, thus giving the doctor a chance to see Troy's symptoms for himself. When Troy did neither, she took the doctor aside and tried to explain the situation, insisting that he do something. The doctor assured her that Troy was in the best of health, showed no sign of allergies or sinus problems, and was probably just "going through a stage" in which he had developed some harmless tics. Donna was embarrassed to have made such a fuss about what was apparently a minor problem.

Almost as soon as Donna and Troy got back into the car, Troy's throat-clearing began again, and the blinking resumed by the time they were home.

Frustrated, Troy's parents decided to attack the problem in another way. They made sure Troy was tucked into bed every night at eight so he got plenty of sleep. Hoping to "calm him down," they removed all caffeine from his diet, including chocolate, and refused to allow him to watch any violent or overly exciting television programs or videos.

> **tics**: Involuntary, repeated actions or sounds.

Instead of showing improvement, Troy began yet another habit: a rhythmic grunting from deep in the back of his throat.

Then things got worse. One afternoon Troy came home from the bus stop in tears. In response to Donna's anxious questions, he finally sobbed out the story of what had happened. Other second-graders had begun calling him names and made fun of his habits by imitating them behind the teacher's back. Worst of all, when Troy invited his best friend Zach to walk home from the bus stop with him that day, Zach refused. "My mother says I can't play with you anymore," Zach said. "She says there's something wrong with you and you're acting weird."

Donna called the pediatrician again but got the same reassurances. "You just wait a few months, Mrs. Sheridan," he told her. "He'll probably grow out of it." She didn't bring the subject up with him again.

After the day his friends made fun of him, Troy struggled to stop his tics. He found he could control them to a certain degree during the school day, and he learned different ways to hide them when they became uncontrollable. When the urge to do the blinking, grunting, or coughing became too strong to resist, he would ask to go to the restroom, where he could do this behavior in private, sometimes for five or ten minutes at a time. By the time he got home, however, Troy was so tense from suppressing the tics that he blinked, coughed, and grunted almost constantly for several hours.

As he entered middle school and then high school, Troy grew increasingly ashamed of his odd behavior. He noticed that the urge to perform the tics grew uncontrollably strong when he was tense or excited, so he avoided talking to girls or going to sporting events. Secretly, Troy wanted nothing more than to try out for the school play, but he knew that the tension of being on stage could make his tics even more pronounced. Troy was growing sadder and lonelier each year, and he sometimes felt as though he were in solitary confinement, imprisoned by his uncontrollable urges.

Even though Troy's pediatrician didn't think his symptoms were serious, most doctors today would recognize that Troy suffers from Tourette's syndrome, one of the tic disorders. The tic disorders encompass a large variety of motor and vocal behaviors. Tics can be simple, meaning that they involve only a few muscles or simple sounds; or they can be complex, involving multiple groups of muscles, or groups of words, or sentences.

According to the DSM-IV-TR, a tic is defined as:

sudden, rapid, recurrent, nonrhythmic, stereotyped movement or vocalization. . . . Examples of simple motor tics are eye blinking, nose wrinkling, neck jerking, shoulder shrugging, facial grimacing, and abdominal tensing. . . . Complex motor tics include hand gestures, jumping, touching, pressing, stomping, facial contortions, repeatedly smelling an object, squatting, deep knee bends, retracing steps, twirling when walking, and assuming and holding unusual postures. . . . Copropraxia (a sudden, tic-like vulgar, sexual, or obscene gesture) and mirror phenomena such as echopraxia (involuntary, spontaneous imitation of someone else's movements) are complex motor tics.

Simple vocal tics are meaningless sounds such as throat clearing, grunting, sniffing, snorting, and chirping. Complex vocal tics more clearly involve speech and language and include the sudden, spontaneous expression of single words or phrases; speech blocking; sudden and meaningless changes in the pitch, emphasis, or volume of speech; palilalia (repeating one's own sounds or words); and echolalia (repeating the last-heard sound, word, or phrase). Coprolalia is the sudden, inappropriate expression of a socially unacceptable word or phrase and may include obscenities as well as specific ethnic, racial or religious slurs.

People who have tic disorders usually feel that the urge to perform the tics is irresistible. Even though they can suppress the urge for various amounts of time (as Troy did during the school day), suppression can cause an increasing feeling of tension until the tic is expressed. Then there is a feeling of relief. The DSM-IV-TR explains it this way: "Individuals with tics may feel that the tic is between 'voluntary' and 'involuntary' in that it is often experienced as a giving in to a mounting tension or bodily need, similar to the tension that precedes a sneeze or the almost irresistible need to scratch an itch." Sometimes the individual may have to express the tic over and over, or in just the "right" way, until the tension is relieved.

The category of disorders known as tic disorders includes:

- Tourette's disorder (involves multiple motor tics and one or more vocal tics, with a duration of at least one year)
- chronic motor or vocal tic disorder (involves either motor or vocal tics, but not both, with a duration of at least one year)
- transient tic disorder (involves a single or multiple motor and/or vocal tics, with a duration of at least four weeks, but no more than twelve consecutive months)

- tic disorder not otherwise specified (involves tics that do not fit into the other categories as far as length of duration, or tics that begin after the age of eighteen years)

Individuals who have a tic disorder are often ridiculed and mocked, especially as children. Displaying the symptoms of a tic disorder does not mean that a person is unintelligent, however. Samuel Johnson (1709–1784) was considered one of the most intelligent and educated men of his generation. He wrote the first dictionary for the English language and is one of the most-quoted men in history—and yet biographers and historians speculate that Johnson had some of the symptoms of **obsessive-compulsive disorder**. Some scholars today have decided that he probably suffered from Tourette's disorder as well.

Disorders such as Tourette's do not have black-and-white boundaries but exist on a **continuum**. Tourette's is often accompanied by **dyslexia**, attention-deficit disorder, or obsessive-compulsive disorder. Symptoms can vary from slight vocal and motor tics to jerky movements and very obvious speech difficulties. "Because of the diversity of manifestations, it is increasingly common to talk about the 'Tourette's spectrum' rather than a single Tourette's," writes Elkohnon Goldberg in the foreword to *Twitch and Shout, A Touretter's Tale*, by Lowell Handler.

obsessive compulsive disorder: A personality disorder characterized by preoccupation with perfectionism, control, and orderliness.

continuum: A continuous whole; a thing whose parts cannot be separated or separately discerned.

dyslexia: A learning disability characterized by difficulty in reading, often manifested by reversing letters and words when reading or writing.

A person with a tic disorder may feel like a puppet on a string, with no control over his own movements and expressions.

Autism

Tracy's birth was a long-awaited dream for her parents, Jay and Mary Janoski, who had tried for more than a decade to have a baby. The beautifully decorated nursery in their house was stocked with every possible toy, as well as expensive furnishings and drawers full of new baby clothes.

Tracy was a joy, developing on schedule until late in her first year. Then, Mary began to feel uneasy about some of Tracy's behaviors.

A child with autism may be more interested in building toys that turn or twirl than interacting with human beings.

She never seemed to want to be cuddled or held and even cried at times when she was picked up, which was exactly the opposite of what other babies did. But since Mary could never put into words exactly what it was that seemed strange, she didn't mention her concern to her pediatrician. Instead, she concentrated on the doctor's assurances that Tracy was exactly where she should be on the height and weight charts.

Between the ages of twelve and eighteen months, however, Tracy's behavior became so different from other babies of that age that Mary became convinced that something serious was wrong with her daughter. While her friends' babies seemed to be constantly exploring, touching, pointing, and tasting the things around them, Tracy spent long periods of time crawling around and around a certain spot on the carpet, seemingly unaware of any other human beings. At other times, she sat on the floor and rocked back and forth, back and forth, for an hour or more. Mary watched with longing as her friends' babies began to walk and even run, then develop into affectionate toddlers who readily gave out kisses and hugs. Tracy neither walked nor even pulled herself to a standing position, and she refused to make eye contact with Mary or Jay.

"It's as though I'm invisible to her," Mary told her husband, sobbing as she spoke. "She looks right through me; it's like I'm made of glass."

Mary and Jay scheduled a consultation with Tracy's pediatrician. They listed everything they felt was odd about Tracy's behavior, and the doctor listened carefully. Next, he gave Tracy an intensive physical examination, then met with Mary and Jay again.

"Tracy has autism, or autistic disorder, which we sometimes refer to as AD," he told them. "Doctors and researchers now recognize that the problem is broader than was first thought, so it is also referred to as autistic spectrum disorder, or ASD. Autistic disorder occurs in about one in eighty-eight children, four times as often in boys as in girls. Autism usually becomes evident in the first three years of a child's life, although sometimes it is not diagnosed until he goes to school. Children with autistic disorder seem withdrawn, even self-occupied, and out of touch with reality."

He explained that AD is one of the pervasive developmental disorders, a category that includes:

- Rett's disorder (involves development of multiple specific deficits after a period of normal functioning after birth)
- childhood disintegrative disorder (involves loss of skills after at least two years of seemingly normal development)
- Asperger's disorder (similar to autistic disorder but without significant delays or problems with language or cognitive development)

The doctor gave Mary and Jay plenty of time to ask questions after he finished. "It's not a hopeless situation," he told them at last. "I have a reading list I will give to you that includes several titles by other parents of children with autism. You may be amazed at how much progress they've made with their children."

Defining and understanding the pervasive developmental disorders can be challenging for the parents of children with one of these disorders. Beth Kephart, in her book *A Slant of Sun*, the story of her own son's battle with pervasive developmental disorder not otherwise specified, writes that this disorder is a "label extended to tens of thousands of children. It is a term one hears with increasing frequency; part of the shared lexicon of therapists, recent special-education graduates, bewildered parents. It's an active search on the Internet. But it remains, in my mind, nothing more than a cipher, a way of saying, We are not quite sure what's wrong."

In her book *Exiting Nirvana, a Daughter's Life with Autism*, Clara Claiborne Park comments on the wide range of abilities evident among people with autism, pointing out that "autism has fuzzy margins." Many people

---

lexicon: The vocabulary of a language.

cipher: A method of changing text to conceal its real meaning; a code.

Accepting that their child has a psychiatric disorder like autism is a painful task for parents.

think of a condition like autism as though it could be precisely labeled and diagnosed the same way a germ-caused disease can be. For instance, you either have a cold or you don't; you either have chicken pox or you don't. But autism is not that simple. It is a word that basically stands for a collection of symptoms—but few children with autism will have all the symptoms. Some children with autism may have unique abilities; others may not. When a child does not exactly fit any of the disorders defined by the DSM-IV-TR, she may be labeled as having a pervasive developmental disorder not otherwise specified. This label is a convenient diagnostic label—but it may be confusing to parents.

Park quotes British psychiatrist Lorna Wing, who herself has a daughter with autism, as calling this disorder a "continuum of impairments," then explains her meaning as follows:

> The continuum ranges from the most profoundly physically and mentally retarded person, who has social impairment as one item among a multitude of problems, to the most able, highly intelligent person with social impairment in its subtlest form as his only disability. It overlaps with learning disabilities and shades into eccentric normality. . . . Language, nonverbal communication, reading, writing, calculation, visuo-spatial skills, gross and fine motor-coordination . . . may be intact or delayed or abnormal to any degree of severity in socially impaired people. Any combination of skills and disabilities may be found and any level of overall intelligence.

Although there is a great deal of variation within the symptoms of autism, according to Lorna Wing there are three categories of impairment:

1. impairment in social interaction
2. impairment in communication
3. impairment in imaginative activity

Leo Kanner defined three symptom patterns:

1. failure to use language for communication

A child with autism often enjoys repetitive motions like swinging.

Children with autism were once thought to be possessed by a demon. Today modern medicine has a better understanding of this disorder. However, there is much about autism that still remains a mystery.

2. abnormal development of social reciprocity
3. desire for sameness, as seen in repetitive rituals or intense circumscribed interests

In the months after Tracy was diagnosed as having AD, Mary and Jay became students of their daughter's behavior, determined to understand as much as they could in order to help her. Tracy seemed interested in Mary and Jay only to get things she wanted. "It's as though she uses my arm to reach for a cookie she can't get for herself, but she hardly notices that I, as another human being, am even there," Jay told Mary a few weeks later.

> **reciprocity:** The state of sharing activity of some sort with another person.

They were both dismayed by the tremendous outbursts of temper that began erupting when Tracy was given her meals in any dish other than her Winnie-the-Pooh bowl. They learned to clean the bowl immediately after each meal so that it would be ready for the next one. One by one, they became familiar with the things that distressed Tracy and began to avoid them. At the same time, they read dozens of books on the subject of autism and began to formulate a plan as to how they could best help Tracy grow and develop as much as possible.

Attention-Deficit and Disruptive Behavior Disorders

Carrie Gilette knew almost from the day Danny was born that he was different. She didn't realize just how different, though, until his little brother Jacob was born two years later, and she could compare their behavior.

Even as a toddler, Danny was a whirlwind. The words "sit still" were a foreign language to him. He routinely climbed onto the dining room table or the back of the couch and then launched himself to the floor. He decided at the age of eighteen months to scramble eggs he'd gotten by himself from the refrigerator, and Carrie once found him in the garage, key ring in hand, trying to fit a key into the car ignition. He talked so incessantly that Carrie longed for just thirty seconds of silence. He scattered toys throughout the house but couldn't stand still long enough for Carrie to teach him how to pick them up. When Danny was forced to sit in one place in his car seat, he shook his feet, swung his legs, tapped his hands, then squirmed his body around until he ended up facing over the back of the car seat.

Carrie decided her son needed to learn how to play with other children, so she started a play group at her house on Thursday mornings. At the first meeting, Danny grabbed toys from the other children and charged around the room, banging into the other kids and knocking them over. He shouted and yelled, then threw tantrums when Carrie tried to restrain him. The other mothers left that first play group meeting long before the agreed-upon ending time, and they countered all Carrie's future invitations with creative but firm excuses as to why they couldn't attend anymore.

When Jacob was born, Carrie worried there was something seriously wrong with him. Jacob was content to lie in her arms for long sessions of rocking and cuddling. Later on, he loved nothing better than to curl up on her lap and listen to her read to him. Eventually, Carrie realized that it was Jacob who was the more "normal" child, while Danny's behavior was problematic.

Until that point, Carrie had simply listened to her relatives who, though they all had conflicting views about Danny, didn't seem to think his behavior was abnormal. Some rolled their eyes and said, "He's a piece of work, that boy! You'd better get him under control while you still can." Others shrugged and said, "Oh, don't worry. That's just the way boys are. He'll grow out of it." Carrie had always thought of Danny as simply an excessively busy, highly energetic child. But as she compared him to Jacob, she finally began to realize

A child with attention-deficit/hyperactivity disorder may seem to be constantly active.

Defining the Disorder

Children with ADHD need plenty of opportunities to expend their bountiful supply of energy.

acronym: A word formed from the first, or first few, letters of a series of words.

hyperactivity: Extreme (abnormal) activity.

just how serious his behavior problems were.

Carrie's husband left the family shortly after Danny turned four and Jacob celebrated his second birthday. Left alone to support herself and her children, Carrie knew she had to address Danny's problems before she could get a job that would require putting him into day care. She moved her little family back into her mother's house. Her mother, stretched beyond even a grandmother's patience with Danny's antics, finally shouted, "I think this child has ADHD!" This was the first time Carrie had heard the acronym for attention-deficit/hyperactivity disorder.

She began researching ADHD on the Internet and was amazed at how similar the symptoms sounded to Danny's behavior. Carrie had always taken Danny to her family doctor, but now she made an appointment with a pediatrician, who examined Danny carefully and listened as Carrie recited story after story of her son's behavior. He decided that Danny did indeed have ADHD and gave Carrie more information.

According to the DSM-IV-TR, the essential feature of attention-deficit/hyperactivity disorder is "a persistent pattern of inattention and/or hyperactivity and impulsivity that is more frequently displayed and more severe than is typically observed in individuals at a comparable level of development."

> impulsivity: Tendency to act on sudden impulses.

A child with ADHD may have difficulty focusing on quiet activities like the ones these children are doing.

Children with ADHD often have difficulty coping with academic tasks.

Other features include:

- some hyperactive-impulsive or inattentive symptoms causing impairment before the age of seven
- impairment from the symptoms must be present in at least two places, such as home, school, or work
- symptoms must show evidence of interfering with developmentally appropriate functioning at school, work, or in social occasions.
- symptoms must not be accounted for by other disorders

Symptoms of inattention include:

- failing to pay attention to details; making careless mistakes at work or school
- doing messy work; work done carelessly without considered thought; difficulty sustaining attention and completing tasks
- frequently appearing as if their mind is somewhere else; as if they either are not listening or did not hear
- frequent shifts between unfinished activities; lack of follow-through on schoolwork, chores, other duties
- difficulty organizing tasks and activities
- seeing as aversive tasks requiring sustained mental effort, organizational demands, or close concentration
- work habits that are frequently disorganized (materials for the task are often scattered, lost, carelessly handled, or damaged)
- being easily distracted by trivial noises or events or irrelevant stimuli
- forgetfulness about daily activities, such as forgetting school lunches or missing appointments

> **aversive:** Unpleasant; something to be avoided.

Defining the Disorder

- inattention in conversation, including frequent shifts, not listening, not focusing on the conversation, not following rules of games

Symptoms of hyperactivity include:

- fidgetiness or squirming
- not remaining seated when appropriate
- excessive running or climbing in inappropriate situations
- difficulty playing or engaging quietly in leisure activities
- appearing to be "driven" or "on the go" and getting into everything
- excessive talking
- feelings of restlessness
- tapping hands, shaking legs or feet excessively

Symptoms of impulsivity include:

- impatience
- difficulty delaying responses
- blurting out answers before questions have been finished
- difficulty waiting for one's turn
- frequently interrupting or intruding upon other people (to the degree that it causes difficulties in social, academic, or occupational situations)
- making comments out of turn
- failing to listen to directions
- initiating conversations at inappropriate times
- grabbing objects from others
- clowning around
- actions that may lead to accidents; engaging in potentially dangerous activities without considering possible consequences.

The three types of this disorder are known as:

1. attention-deficit/hyperactivity disorder, combined type. This type is most common for children and adolescents who have the disorder. It includes six or more symptoms of inattention and six or more of hyperactivity-impulsivity symptoms, persisting for at least six months.
2. attention-deficit/hyperactivity disorder, predominantly inattentive type. Involves six or more symptoms of inattention, but fewer than six of hyperactivity-impulsivity, persisting for at least six months.
3. attention-deficit/hyperactivity disorder, predominantly hyperactive-impulsive type. Involves six or more symptoms of hyperactivity-impulsivity, but fewer than six of inattention, persisting for at least six months.

The average age for diagnosis of ADHD is between six and nine years. Symptoms, however, are often present for many years before the child is diagnosed and treated; the typical onset of symptoms happens between three and five years. Not all extremely active preschoolers, however, will later be diagnosed with this disorder.

Intellectual Disabilities

Tina and Zach Davis were enchanted by their newborn daughter; they named her Kelly, after Tina's mother. For the first year of Kelly's life, she progressed a little more slowly than her two older brothers had, but the difference was slight, and her pediatrician didn't mention any concerns.

By the time Kelly was a toddler, however, problems with her development were becoming apparent. Tina and Zach kept hoping their little girl would "catch up" with her big brothers, but during her fifth year she was diagnosed as having an intellectual disability.

Mental Health Services for Children

For many years, children have been a neglected group in the area of mental health services. In the United States, 15 to 19 percent of children under age eighteen have mental health problems. Many more millions are at risk for psychological and developmental disorders. According to research, these at-risk children include fourteen million who live in poverty, seven million who have alcoholic parents, and one million who are neglected and abused.

Twenty to 30 percent of those with mental health problems receive some kind of formal treatment. This, however, leaves a majority who do not. States spent approximately one-fifth as much for treatment of mentally disturbed children as for disturbed adults. Only one percent of psychologists and 10 percent of psychiatrists specialize in childhood disorders.

In recent decades, the government has begun to address this problem. The Federal Child and Adolescent Service Program (1984) authorized funds to help states develop integrated mental health programs for children. The Amendment to the Education of the Handicapped Act (1986) authorized services for preschoolers at risk for developmental delays. A new family support service has been available for the last decade for at-risk children. Known as "home visiting," trained home visitors provide counseling, problem solving, and casework services.

Adapted from Perrotto and Culkin, *Exploring Abnormal Psychology*.

Then, to Tina and Zach's dismay, Kelly began to exhibit self-destructive behavior, sometimes biting at her arms and hands.

Kelly was classed as having a moderate intellectual disability. The pediatrician and family counselor both assured the Davis family that this meant she could be educated, probably up to the second-grade level. Their local school district had a program for children like Kelly, and they enrolled her as soon as she was old enough. At times, Kelly seemed very happy in the special classes, but at other times, her behavior was disruptive. Her behavior of biting at her arms, especially, was a hurdle that had to be overcome before Kelly could consistently attend classes and continue to learn. Tina and Zach were committed to doing whatever was necessary to keep Kelly in her classes, since they could see progress when she was able to attend regularly. They asked for a joint meeting with Kelly's pediatrician, her teachers, and the family counselor to decide the best way of working on the problem of keeping Kelly in school.

Mental retardation, a term often used for intellectual disabilities in medical literature, is defined by Richard S. Perrotto and Joseph Culkin in *Exploring Abnormal Psychology* as "significantly subaverage intellectual functioning" (a score of seventy or less on a standardized IQ test) "and deficits in adaptive behavior appearing in the developmental period." The onset of this disorder must be prior to the age of eighteen. The presenting symptoms are usually the individual's difficulty in coping with common life demands, or **adaptive functioning**, rather than a low IQ. Education, motivation, personality characteristics, and social and vocational opportunities all may influence adaptive functioning. Problems with adaptive func-

> **adaptive functioning:** Coping with common life demands and meeting the standards of personal independence expected of someone in a particular age range.

custodial: Watching over and protecting someone.

tioning are more likely to respond to remedial efforts than will problems based on a subaverage IQ.

From one to three percent of the population is thought to have intellectual disabilities, but this group includes great diversity. Many individuals considered to have intellectual disabilities live self-sufficient lives, working and even raising families. Others, however, are seriously handicapped and need care and supervision at all times.

Approximately 85 percent of people diagnosed as mentally retarded fall into the category of "mild retardation." This means they are considered able to achieve up to a sixth-grade level of education and are able to learn many of the skills of independent living, as well as perform unskilled or semiskilled work. Most people with intellectual disabilities progress through all the normal developmental stages; they simply do it more slowly than people without intellectual disabilities. An estimated three-fourths of all people with intellectual disabilities are under the age of eighteen, but as they mature, about two-thirds of this group lose this diagnosis as they enter adulthood.

Mental retardation is categorized according to degree of severity:

1. MILD MENTAL RETARDATION. With an IQ level of 50 or 55 to approximately 70, this group comprises about 85 percent of all people with mental retardation; they are considered educable up to the sixth-grade level; they can learn many independent living skills and accomplish unskilled/semiskilled work.
2. MODERATE MENTAL RETARDATION. With IQ levels of 35 or 40 to 50 or 55, these individuals comprise about 10 percent of people with mental retardation; they are considered educable up to a second-grade level; they can learn semi-independent living skills and can be trained for unskilled work.

3. SEVERE MENTAL RETARDATION. At this level, IQs range from 20 or 25 to 35 or 40. This group comprises from three to four percent of people with mental retardation; they can be trained to perform simple self-care, but they need close supervision and may be suitable for group home living.
4. PROFOUND MENTAL RETARDATION. With IQ levels below 20 or 25, this group comprises from 1 to 2 percent of people with mental retardation; they can be educated up to a preschool level, and they can learn only minimal self-care and language; they frequently have physical handicaps and custodial care is required.

> **hypothyroidism:** Inadequate levels of the thyroid hormone in blood levels.
>
> **toxins:** Substances that are poisonous.

Causes of Intellectual Disabilities

Possible causes of intellectual disabilities include:
- inherited (genetic) disorders or chromosome defects
- abuse of certain drugs or alcohol during pregnancy
- specific infections during pregnancy
- malnutrition before and after birth during essential periods of brain development
- complications from being born prematurely
- severe bleeding at birth
- birth injury or lack of oxygen during delivery
- glandular problems (for example, hypothyroidism)
- toxins that affect the brain (for example, lead poisoning)
- accidents that cause brain damage

Since so many of these causes have their roots in pregnancy and delivery, adequate medical care and nutrition is essential throughout all pregnancies.

congenital: A condition that exists from birth.

Chromosome Problems as a Cause of Intellectual Disabilities

Human cells normally contain forty-six chromosomes (except sperm and egg cells, which have twenty-three each). These chromosomes are arranged in pairs; the twenty-third pair contains the sex chromosomes, X (female) and Y (male). At conception, mistakes can happen and too much or too little chromosome material can be included. The child's characteristics will depend on which chromosome was affected. This sort of mistake can be inherited, and it may occur more frequently to children born of older parents. However, scientists do not yet understand completely why these chromosomal irregularities happen.

Down Syndrome

A Down syndrome child has an extra chromosome (called a trisomy) on the twenty-first pair of chromosomes; in other words, he has forty-seven instead of forty-six chromosomes. This is the most common cause of intellectual disabilities, accounting for about 30 percent of all cases of this disorder. Approximately 1 out of every 800 to 1,000 live births will be a Down syndrome child.

Down syndrome children have a distinctive appearance. The backs of their heads are flat, and they have slanted eyes with skin folds at the inner corners. (This is why they were once referred to as Mongoloids, since people thought they looked like people from the Asian country of Mongolia.) They have small noses and ears and unusually tiny hands and feet. Their muscle strength is less than the average child's their age.

About one third of these children also have congenital heart disease. Sometimes they are born with other physical defects, such as bowel blockage. In the past, this meant that many Down syndrome children did not live to grow up, but now their life expectancy is usually from fifty to sixty years.

The level of intelligence varies from child to child; an individual with Down syndrome can range in functioning from severe intellectual disabilities to low average. Children with Down syndrome tend to be sociable and affectionate, but each individual is unique.

> **symmetry:** Similarity on either side of the center line.
>
> **apnea:** A temporary stoppage of breathing, sometimes during sleep.
>
> **seizures:** Sudden attacks of pain, disease, or convulsions.

Fragile-X Syndrome

This is the second most common genetic cause of intellectual disabilities. Fragile X syndrome affects about 1 out every 4,000 males and 1 out of every 6,000 to 8,000 females.

One of the X chromosomes of individuals with this syndrome will appear to be weak or fragile looking. Because girls are protected by having two X chromosomes (while boys have an X and a Y), this syndrome is usually seen only in males. They are mildly to severely retarded with abnormal facial features, which include large jaws, foreheads, and ears. They are often hyperactive and resist changes in their environments; they may have attention deficits and problems articulating words; about 20 to 40 percent will show symptoms of autism. Girls who carry this chromosome may have learning disorders or mild retardation.

Cri Du Chat Syndrome

This is another genetic cause of intellectual disabilities, but it is much more rare, occurring in only 1 out of every 200,000 to 500,000 live births. Children with this disorder make a distinctive noise that sounds like a cat's cry, and they are usually severely retarded. They are small and grow slowly, with small, round heads and faces that

hypertension: High blood pressure.

toxemia: The spreading of poisonous bacteria through the blood.

placenta previa: A condition of pregnancy in which the placenta is attached to the lower section of the uterus.

lack symmetry. Their eyes are wide set, with skin folds on the inner lids. These children usually learn to walk, but their language development is generally poor.

Trisomy 18 and Trisomy 13

Children with these syndromes have extra material in their eighteenth or thirteenth chromosomes. Again, these disorders are very rare. The children born with either of these disorders will be profoundly retarded, but most do not live past their first year. They are small and weak, and most have other medical problems as well; for instance, they may have congenital heart disease, **apnea**, or **seizures**.

Intrauterine Causes of Intellectual Disabilities

These are causes of intellectual disabilities that occur during pregnancy, when the child is still in the mother's uterus. The three most common are:

1. FETAL ALCOHOL SYNDROME. This occurs when the mother exposes her unborn child to high levels of alcohol. It results in mild intellectual disabilities with many symptoms of attention-deficit/hyperactivity disorder as well. Children with this syndrome tend to be small, with narrow "cat" eyes, flat cheeks, a short

nose, and thin upper lip. This syndrome occurs in as many as 1 out of every 600 live births.
2. ASPHYXIA. This occurs when the baby does not get enough oxygen within its mother's uterus. It can be caused by the mother's hypertension, toxemia, or placenta previa.
3. INFECTIONS. Two of the most common are rubella (measles), and toxoplasmosis, a disease often caught from cats and birds.

Because other mental disorders coexist with intellectual disabilities in 30 to 70 percent of retardation cases, psychiatric drugs are sometimes necessary to help the patient to be able to respond to behavioral therapy or other treatments. Anxiety disorders are a good example of this. According to researchers, a broad range of anxiety disorders exists along with intellectual disabilities in about 25 percent of patients studied. Researchers point to the psychosocial stress factors among this population—such as fragile self-esteem, fears of falling, and loss of caregivers—as possible factors contributing to both the development and expression of anxiety disorders. Psychiatric medications can help control or alleviate the symptoms of anxiety disorders and make it possible for patients to receive care for problems related to their intellectual disabilities.

Earlier in history, people commonly thought that children and adolescents with mental disorders had no hope of change. Many of those who showed signs of intellectual disabilities, for example, were simply put in institutions for long periods of time, some for life. Now, however, it is obvious that, given the proper care and treatment, many of these individuals can be educated, trained to care for themselves, and go on to contribute in some way to the world around them.

Researchers work to discover new drugs to treat psychiatric disorders.

Chapter Two

History of the Drugs

Drugs are discovered and developed in many different ways, and their stories make for interesting reading. Drugs are often discovered when researchers are studying a particular disease, looking for a way to combat or cure it. However, the story behind the development of psychiatric drugs has been quite different, according to Jack M. Gorman, M.D., in *The Essential Guide to Psychiatric Drugs*. Antipsychotic drugs, for example, were discovered for the most part by anesthesiologists. When they administered these drugs in order to anesthetize surgical patients, they observed the calming effect the drugs had.

The best known example involves Henri Laborit, a surgeon in Paris. In 1952, Laborit was puzzling over a way to reduce surgical shock in his patients, caused for the most part by anesthesia. He felt that if he could use less anesthesia during surgery, his patients

Before the discovery of psychiatric medications, many treatments for psychiatric disorders were bizarre—like this circulating swing that was once used to treat "insanity."

SHOWING HOW BANDS AND CHAINS IN THE PAST WERE MISTAKENLY USED AS AUXILIARIES TO CURE.

A person with a psychiatric disorder might once have been treated with shackles to "cure" him.

could recover more quickly. Since shock was known to result from certain brain chemicals, he decided to try using another chemical to counteract this effect. He tried antihistamines, drugs that are usually used to fight allergies.

Laborit noticed that when he gave his patients a strong dose of antihistamines, they no longer seemed anxious about their upcoming surgery. As a result, Laborit could use much less anesthesia during the operation. The effect of the antihistamines was even more far-reaching than what Laborit originally intended, affecting his patients' mental state so strongly that the doctor began to think these drugs—especially chlorpromazine—might be of some use in the field of psychiatry.

sedative: Having a calming effect.

behaviorism: A type of psychology that focuses on reinforcing specific observable behaviors.

The climate in psychiatry at that time, however, dictated that electric shock or various psychotherapies were the treatments of choice. "No one in his right mind in psychiatry was working with drugs," Canadian psychiatrist Heinz Lehmann says of that period. But one colleague of Laborit's told his brother-in-law, psychiatrist Pierre Deniker, what had happened with the chlorpromazine. Deniker ordered some of the drug to try on his most agitated, uncontrollable patients.

Deniker was amazed by the results. Patients who had been restrained because of their violent behavior and those who had stood in one spot without moving for weeks could now be left without supervision and could actually respond to other people.

Severe mental illness had been growing in America between the years of 1904, when two out of a thousand people were institutionalized in mental hospitals, and 1955, when the number had risen to four out of a thousand. There was really nothing available to help the mentally ill, and they were routinely "warehoused" in state institutions. At the same time, an American drug company named SmithKline was hoping to expand its line of drugs. SmithKline heard about chlorpromazine, bought the rights to it from a European company called Rhone-Poulenc, and marketed it in the United States as Thorazine, an antivomiting medication. SmithKline tried to convince American medical schools and university psychology departments to test the drug for psychiatric use, but chlorpromazine was considered just another **sedative**. Academics and doctors were still interested in treating mental disorders solely with psychoanalysis and **behaviorism**.

SmithKline then asked Dr. Deniker to help influence doctors in America to use the drug, and he did so. The first successes for chlorpromazine came in state institutions, where test results seemed

Brand Name vs. Generic Name

Talking about psychiatric drugs can be confusing, because every drug has at least two names: its "generic name" and the "brand name" that the pharmaceutical company uses to market the drug. Generic names come from the drugs' chemical structure, while brand names are used by drug companies in order to inspire public recognition and loyalty for their products.

Here are the brand names and generic names for some common psychiatric drugs:

- Anafranil®   clomipramine hydrochloride
- Haldol®   haloperidol
- Klonopin®   clonazepam
- Paxil®   paroxetine hydrochloride
- Prozac®   fluoxetine hydrochloride
- Risperdal®   risperidone
- Ritalin®   methylphenidate hydrochloride
- Tofranil®   imipramine hydrochloride
- Valium®   diazepam
- Xanax®   alprazolam
- Zoloft®   sertraline hydrochloride

schizophrenia: A psychological disorder characterized by a break with reality. Symptoms can include hallucinations and delusions.

hallucinations: Perceptions of objects with no basis in reality.

delusions: False beliefs based on an incorrect perception of reality.

miraculous. When chlorpromazine was approved by the U. S. Food and Drug Administration in 1954, it had a huge effect on thousands, even millions, of people with mental disorders. It decreased the intensity of **schizophrenia** symptoms such as **hallucinations** and **delusions**. It calmed people without sedating them, and in many cases, it allowed them to lead an almost normal life. By 1964, fifty million people around the world had taken the drug, and SmithKline had doubled their revenues three times.

Although side effects and other drawbacks associated with chlorpromazine even-

Centuries ago a child or adolescent diagnosed with psychiatric problems might have been caged.

tually came to light, the dramatic effects this chemical had on the brain led people to think differently about brain function and behavior.

For instance, since one side effect of chlorpromazine was to produce effects similar to those of Parkinson's disease, researchers began considering the possibility that similar chemicals might be involved in natural Parkinson's disease and that it might be possible to counteract them. This type of thinking eventually resulted in understanding the role of dopamine and other **neurotransmitters** (see chapter three for an explanation of how neurotransmitters work in the central nervous system), an advance that has had great impact on the treatment of mental disorders. When the antipsychotic drugs were observed to relieve **psychotic** symptoms, researchers found that their effect was due to the drug's ability to block dopamine receptors in the brain. As a result, scientists began to wonder if schizophrenia, or any part of it, could be a result of an excess of dopamine. Operating on the same principle, scientists then questioned whether depression could be related to a lack of the neurotransmitters serotonin and noradrenaline, and if anxiety could be caused by a lack of GABA (a neurotransmitter called gamma-aminobutyric acid).

> **neurotransmitters:** Chemicals found in the bloodstream that assist in the sending of impulses from neuron to neuron.
>
> **psychotic:** Having to do with a loss of contact with reality.

After chlorpromazine, drug companies went on to develop and market other medicines to treat psychiatric problems. More antipsychotics were developed after chlorpromazine, including haloperidol (Haldol), the most thoroughly researched antipsychotic drug used to treat autism. The effectiveness of haloperidol in treatment of autism has been demonstrated both in long- and short-term studies, but concerns about haloperidol and the possibility of related **dyskinesias** have led to increased interest in the newer, **atypical** antipsychotics developed after 1985. Risperidone (Risperdal) is one of these atypical antipsychotics. Studies are still under way, but initial reports show that this drug may be useful in treating autism and may have fewer side effects than haloperidol. Risperidone is frequently used in treating Tourette's and other tic disorders.

The benzodiazepines (such as Valium and Xanax) are commonly used to decrease anxiety, but at least one of these medications, clonazepam (Klonopin), has now been proven effective in the treatment of tic disorders.

In the last half of the twentieth century, researchers developed many drugs for the treatment of depression, including the tricyclic antidepressants (TCAs) such as imipramine (Tofranil) in the 1960s and fluoxetine (Prozac), sertraline (Zoloft), and paroxetine (Paxil), all **selective serotonin reuptake inhibitors** (SSRIs), in the 1980s. Some of these medications are also proving valuable to those with childhood and adolescent disorders. While Tofranil is used to treat depression and anxiety disorders, it is also used for ADHD. The SSRIs clomipramine and fluvoxamine have proven to be useful for many disorders, including autistic disorder.

Methylphenidate hydrochloride, one of the stimulant classes of drugs, was introduced under the name Ritalin in the early 1960s. It became the preferred drug for calming hyperactivity, replacing psychostimulants such as benzedrine. There has been a great deal of controversy about the use of Ritalin. (For more on this subject, see chapter six, Risks and Side Effects.)

---

dyskinesias: Difficulties in making voluntary movements.

atypical: Not the usual; unexpected.

selective serotonin reuptake inhibitors: A class of drugs that interferes with the movement of serotonin in the brain.

In order to develop new drugs that affect the brain, scientists know they need a better understanding of how the brain works. The advances made in recent years in imaging living, intact brains have impacted this understanding in important ways. While it is relatively simple to tell what is going on in other body organs by means of a blood test, information about the brain is not so easily accessible. Because of what scientists refer to as the blood-brain barrier, many medi-

blood-brain barrier: The barrier created by the walls of the brain's capillaries that prevents most proteins and drugs from passing from the blood into the brain tissue and cerebrospinal fluid.

Because of the blood-brain barrier, many psychiatric drugs cannot enter the brain. This means that psychiatric medications need to be specially designed to get past this barrier in order to treat the particular disorder.

Drug Approval

Before a drug can be marketed in the United States, it must be officially approved by the Food and Drug Administration (FDA). Today's FDA is the primary consumer protection agency in the United States. Operating under the authority given it by the government, and guided by laws established throughout the twentieth century, the FDA has established a rigorous drug approval process that verifies the safety, effectiveness, and accuracy of labeling for any drug marketed in the United States.

While the United States has the FDA for the approval and regulation of drugs and medical devices, Canada has a similar organization called the Therapeutic Product Directorate (TPD). The TPD is a division of Health Canada, the Canadian government department of health. The TPD regulates drugs, medical devises, disinfectants, and sanitizers with disinfectant claims. Some of the things that the TPD monitors are quality, effectiveness, and safety. Just as the FDA must approve new drugs in the United States, the TPD must approve new drugs in Canada before those drugs can enter the market.

cines are not able to get into the brain. Now, however, the following valuable methods for "seeing" the brain have been developed:

- CAT (computerized axial tomography) scans reveal brain structures without harming the patient.
- MRI (magnetic resonance imaging) gives highly refined pictures of the brain using magnetic fields and without using radiation.
- PET (positron emission tomography) and SPECT (single-photon emission computed tomography) reveal brain structure and also show metabolic activity in various parts of the brain (brain chemicals and their receptors).

With the development of these last tests, scientists can now inject chemicals labeled with tiny amounts of **radioactivity** into a person's bloodstream and watch where in the brain they go and to what they bind. These imaging techniques are used to see abnormalities in the brains of people with autism, Tourette's, **panic disorder**, depression, obsessive-compulsive disorder, schizophrenia, and other mental disorders. They are also helping scientists learn more about the receptors for antipsychotic and benzodiazepine antianxiety drugs.

Research continues on other fronts as well. With the advent of genetic research, molecular geneticists have linked some psychiatric diseases, such as schizophrenia and bipolar disorder, to abnormal genes. Other researchers have developed methods to study psychotherapies under controlled conditions. This means that psychotherapies and drug therapies can now be compared scientifically, so that practitioners will soon have a better understanding of the uses and the limitations of both types of treatment.

Although the discovery of psychiatric drugs began by accident, researchers and pharmaceutical companies have used the knowledge gained from those early discoveries to develop many helpful medications. Research in this field is ongoing, and new drugs are being tested all the time.

When used properly, psychiatric medications can make a tremendous difference in the life of many children and adolescents diagnosed with mental disorders.

radioactivity: The capability of certain elements to spontaneously emit energy particle by disintegrating the nucleus.

panic disorder: Recurrent pattern of attacks of extreme fear or discomfort, altering with at least a month or more of concern about those attacks.

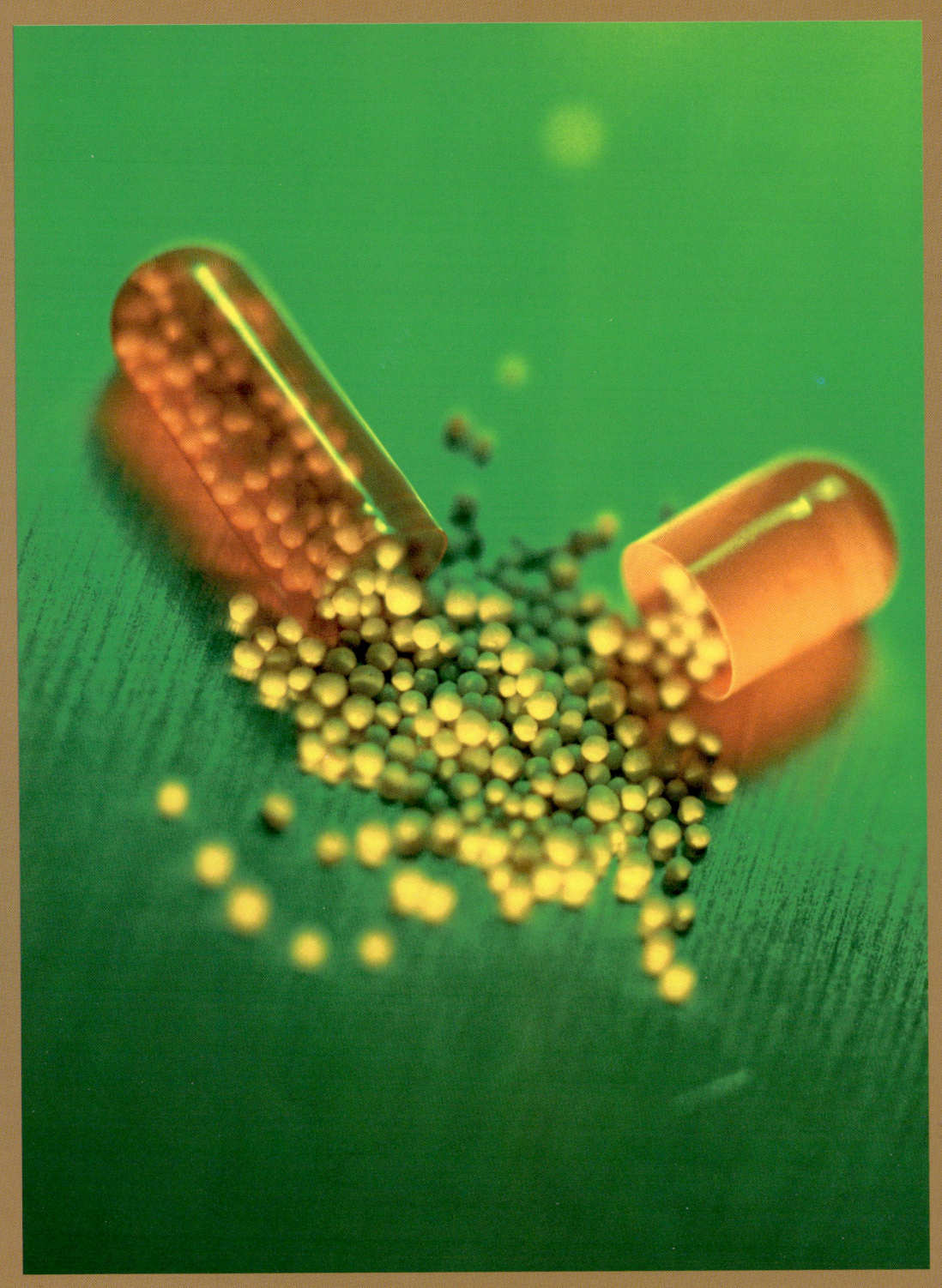

Psychiatric drugs are powerful chemicals with the ability to affect brain function.

Chapter Three

How Does the Drug Work?

Although Troy continued to suppress his tics as much as possible when he was with other students, he found himself overwhelmed by the need to perform the tics as soon as he was alone. One day he went to the school clinic with a bad headache. The nurse instructed him to lie down in a separate room near her office; she went to check on him in half an hour. Unaware that she was standing in the doorway, Troy was both blinking and grunting. He was also shrugging his right shoulder repeatedly, another tic that had developed over the years.

The nurse watched silently for a few seconds, and then purposely made noise as she entered the room so that Troy would know she was there. The tics stopped immediately. The nurse, however, had experience with Tourette's patients. When Troy's headache was better, she discussed Tourette's with him, explaining that the disorder was named for French neurologist Dr. Georges Gilles de la Tourette, who first reported a case in 1825. Troy's cheeks flushed red when she explained that she had seen the tics he exhibited when he thought he was alone. He refused to look at her.

"Troy, this is not something you should be embarrassed about," she said gently. "After years and years of study, researchers think Tourette's is caused by a gene inherited from one of your parents. It's three to four times more likely to show up in boys than in girls, and while we can't be absolutely sure how many other people have

In earlier times, someone with Tourette's disorder might be sent to the church, so that a priest could cast out the "demon."

When Psychiatric Medicines May Be Needed

When a patient exhibits:

- suicidal thoughts
- presence of hallucinations or delusions
- decrease in ability to function (includes inability to sleep, eat, work, care for children, perform personal hygiene)
- self-destructive behavior
- uncontrollable compulsions (constant washing or checking)

Adapted from *The New Psychiatry*, by Jack M. Gorman, M.D.

Tourette's, because it often goes undiagnosed, estimates are that at least two hundred thousand people in the United States have this disorder."

Finally, Troy looked up at the nurse. "Are you saying that Tourette's is what I have?"

"I'm not qualified to make an official diagnosis, but I'd like you to see a doctor who can. He may be able to help you get these tics under control."

"There's no controlling them!" Troy burst out. "I've been trying for eight years now, and it's impossible. Or maybe it's just me. Maybe I don't have any self-control."

"I don't think self-control is the answer," she told him. "And I suspect that you have plenty of it, anyway. I've seen you around school, in the hall and at your locker, and I've never seen a sign of these tics before. I can only imagine how much self-control it takes to not perform those tics in front of other people."

"I don't know why I try, anyway!" Troy burst out. "Sometimes I can't hold them in no matter how hard I try, and then everybody makes fun of me. If they ever saw me when I'm alone, they'd think I'm crazy."

"Well, since you've worked so long and so hard to solve this problem, would you be willing to try just one more thing for me? Would you let me schedule an appointment for you and your parents with the doctor? All you'll have to do is answer some questions and talk to him."

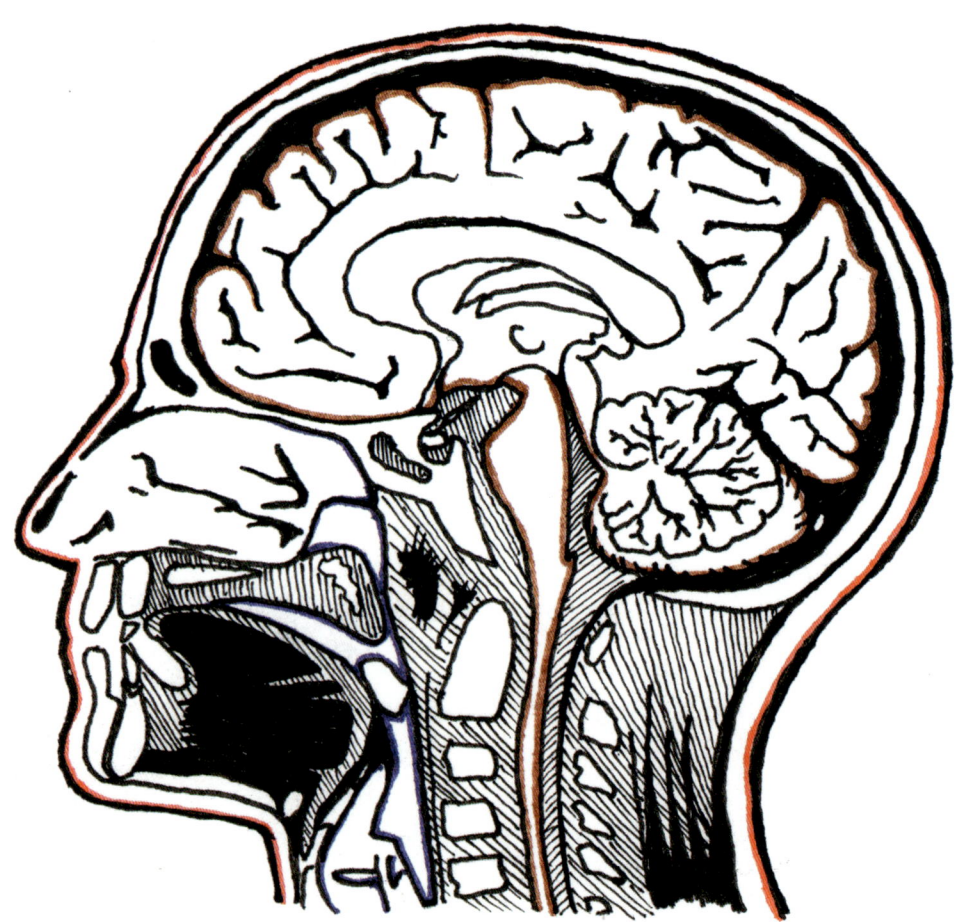

The human brain is amazingly complex.

Troy agreed to one visit, and the nurse called his parents to give them the information and make sure they would attend the appointment with him. "I want to start you on risperidone, one of the atypical antipsychotics, to help you control the tics," Dr. Johnson told him, "It's important that you have at least some understanding of how the medicine will work." He gave Troy a brief explanation and then advised him to begin researching his disorder so that he could find out even more.

Troy read that Tourette's is directly connected to the neurotransmitter dopamine, one of the major biochemical systems in the brain. The disorder is also connected to brain structures called the basal ganglia, which are critical for the initiation of movement and more complex behaviors. Some scientists believe that in Tourette's the basal ganglia somehow escape the control normally exerted over them by the prefrontal cortex.

Troy realized he had a great deal more to learn about the human brain. He began researching and learned some amazing things.

The sheer complexity of the human brain is astounding. Inside the brain are millions and millions of neurons—specialized brain cells that are capable of passing on messages to other neurons. There are so many neurons in our brains that if all the neurons with their axons from a single human brain were stretched out end to end it would go to the moon and back.

The brain does not operate alone, though. It is part of the central nervous system (CNS), which also includes the spinal cord. Between the brain and the central nervous system, each individual has billions of neurons, both sensory and motor. Our five senses—sight, hearing, smell, touch, and taste—feed information from the outside world to the brain by way of the sensory neurons. Motor neurons respond to this information by making the muscles of our bodies move.

> prefrontal cortex: The part of the brain responsible for intentional, goal-driven behavior, planning, and critical judgment.

How does this vast communication system work in real life? Let's say that Justin, who is too young to understand the dangers of fire, is toasting a piece of bread in the toaster. Unfortunately, the toaster jams, and the bread begins to smoke. Justin gives the toaster a tap, and the charred slice of bread pops into view. Now the bread actually bursts into flame. Justin reaches out—and the fire comes in contact with Justin's finger, stimulating a nerve cell there.

In a flash, the nerve cell in Justin's finger conducts a message about the situation along its axons to the spinal cord. There, information is relayed to other neurons that send information back to Justin's hand, telling it to move. Fast.

However, that's not the end of the message relay going on just then in Justin's body. If Justin doesn't learn from this experience that fire can hurt, his little finger could face the same kind of danger again in the future. So the information that fire is hot—and that he should keep his hand away from it—is relayed to yet other neurons, and this important information is stored in Justin's memory.

Neurons are irreplaceable. While other areas of the body, such as skin or hair, replace dead cells with new cells of the same type, the brain is different. It has always been thought that once the brain or the spinal cord is injured, those injuries are permanent. Apparently, once neurons die, the body does not make new neurons. However, some scientists are now questioning this.

How do messages, or neural impulses, travel through the body to the spine or brain? Much of the answer lies in the structure of the neuron itself. In one area of each neuron, the cell body sends out dendrites, projections that look like tiny twigs. In another area of the neuron, the cell body extends a long, thin filament called an axon. At the end of the axon are several terminal buttons. The terminal buttons lie on the dendrites of another neuron, so that each neuron functions as a link in the communication chain. The chain does not run in just one direction, however. Because each neuron is in contact with many other neurons, the CNS is like a vast mesh or web of interconnected groups of neurons. The connections and interconnections possible between these millions of neurons—with their cell bodies, axons, and dendrites—is amazing!

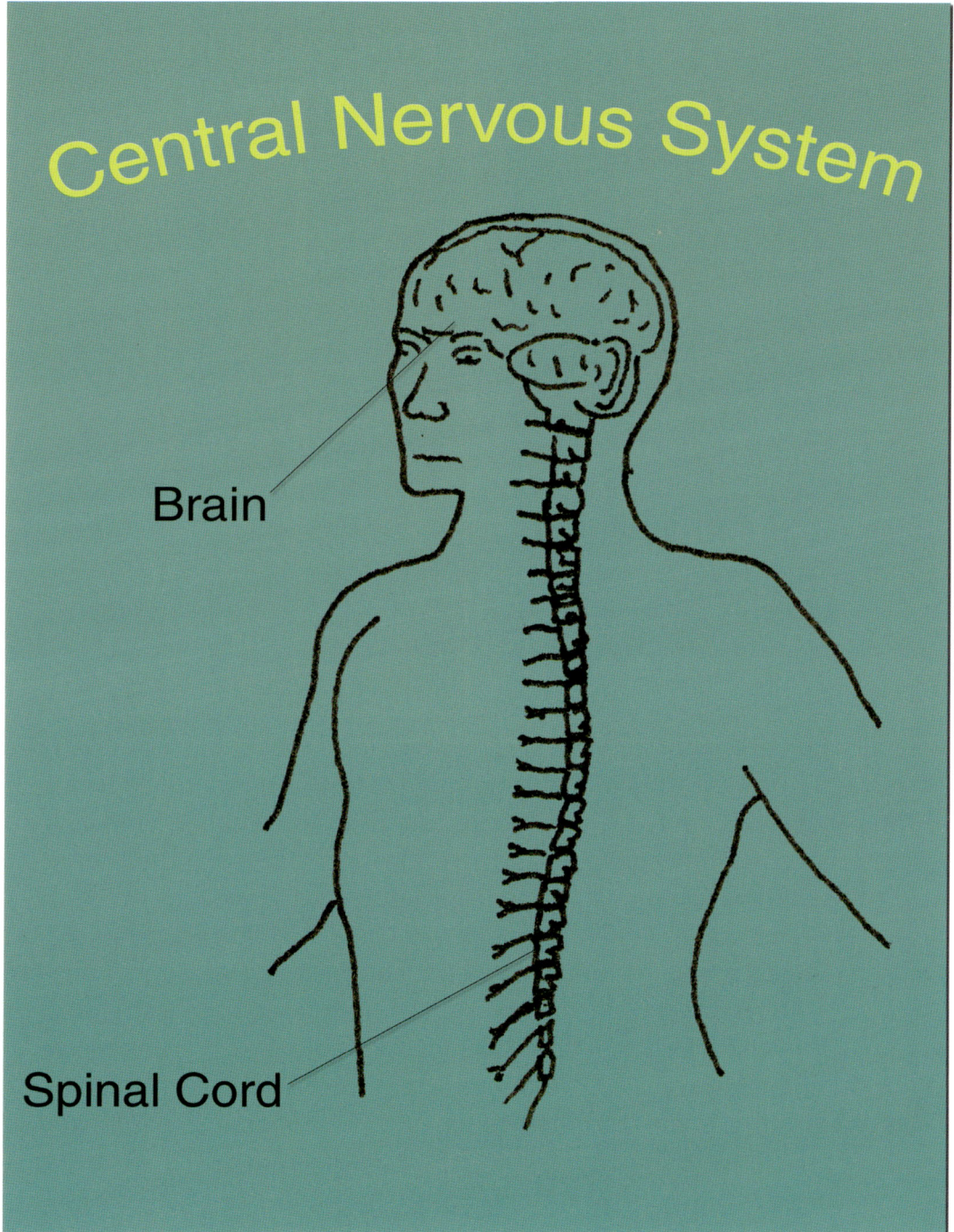

The central nervous system consists of a vast network of neurons, which send messages to and from the brain and spinal cord.

When Either Psychiatric Medicines or Psychotherapy May Work

When a patient exhibits:

- depression that does not include suicidal thoughts, loss of function, or inability to eat or sleep
- panic disorder
- generalized anxiety disorder
- social phobia
- bulimia

Adapted from *The New Psychiatry*, by Jack M. Gorman, M.D.

Brain cells communicate by sending electrical signals from neuron to neuron. Although axons and dendrites do not actually touch other neurons, they lie very close together. In between cells is a tiny space called a synapse, and it is through this space that nerve impulses travel, jumping the space in much the same way an electric current would. When a message is to be transferred, a neuron "fires," and its terminal buttons release chemicals called neurotransmitters (biochemical substances such as norepinephrine and dopamine), which make jumping the synapse possible. When an electrical signal comes to the end of one neuron, the cell fires, secreting the proper neurotransmitter into the synapse. This chemical messenger then crosses from the presynaptic neuron (the brain cell sending the message) to the postsynaptic neuron (the brain cell receiving the message), where it binds itself to the appropriate chemical receptor and influences the behavior of this second neuron. Neurotransmitters can influence the behavior of the post-synaptic neuron by either transmitting the message or by inhibiting the passage of the message.

When the neurotransmitter binds to the receptors, other processes are set in motion in the postsynaptic brain cell, either exciting it to keep sending the message along or inhibiting it to stop the transmission of the message. After the impulse is passed from one neuron to another, the neurotransmitter falls off the receptor and back into the synapse. There it is either taken back into the presynaptic neuron (a kind of neuron recycling), broken down by **enzymes** and discarded to spinal fluid surrounding the brain, or reattaches itself to the receptor, thus strengthening the original signal traveling from the presynaptic neuron.

> **enzymes:** Proteins made by living cells that bring about specific biochemical reactions.

There are at least one hundred billion synapses in the brain. Researchers speculate that there may be hundreds of different neurotransmitters. Many neurons respond to more than one neurotransmitter. It is in this complex brain environment that psychiatric drugs operate, usually by influencing neurotransmitters.

Classes of Drugs and How They Operate

Different classes of drugs operate in different ways. Drugs commonly used to treat childhood and adolescent disorders include tricyclic antidepressants (TCAs), selective serotonin reuptake inhibitors (SSRIs), central nervous system stimulants (CNSSs), and antipsychotics, both standard and atypical. TCAs inhibit the reabsorption of serotonin in the brain and actually increase the amount of serotonin available to brain receptors. (Scientists do not know for certain how TCAs work, but this is the leading theory.) Serotonin is vital for many functions and has been related to depression, anger, and impulsivity. The SSRIs increase the amount of serotonin available to brain receptors but usually work with fewer side effects than do some of the TCAs. Antipsychotics such as haloperidol (Haldol) and pimozide (Orap) work by blocking postsynaptic dopamine receptors and have been effective in treating tics and, in some cases, the self-injurious and aggressive behaviors often associated with autism and sometimes with intellectual disabilities. The atypical antipsychotic risperidone (Risperdal) is thought to block the ability of both dopamine and serotonin to bind to their receptors.

Specific Drugs Used for Childhood and Adolescent Pervasive Developmental Disorders (PDD)

Drugs most commonly used to treat PDD include the standard antipsychotics, such as chlorpromazine (Thorazine), which block postsynaptic dopamine receptors; atypical antipsychotics, such as risperidone (Risperdal), which block a subset of dopamine and serotonin receptors; and centrally acting alpha-agonists, such as clonidine (Catapres), which stimulate postsynaptic alpha adrenergic receptors.

alpha-agonist: A chemical substance capable of combining with a receptor on a cell, causing the cell to react in some way.

Tic Disorders

Commonly used drugs for tic disorders include the standard antipsychotics haloperidol (Haldol) and pimozide (Orap), clonidine (Catapres), and TCAs such as imipramine (Tofranil) and nortriptyline (Pamelor).

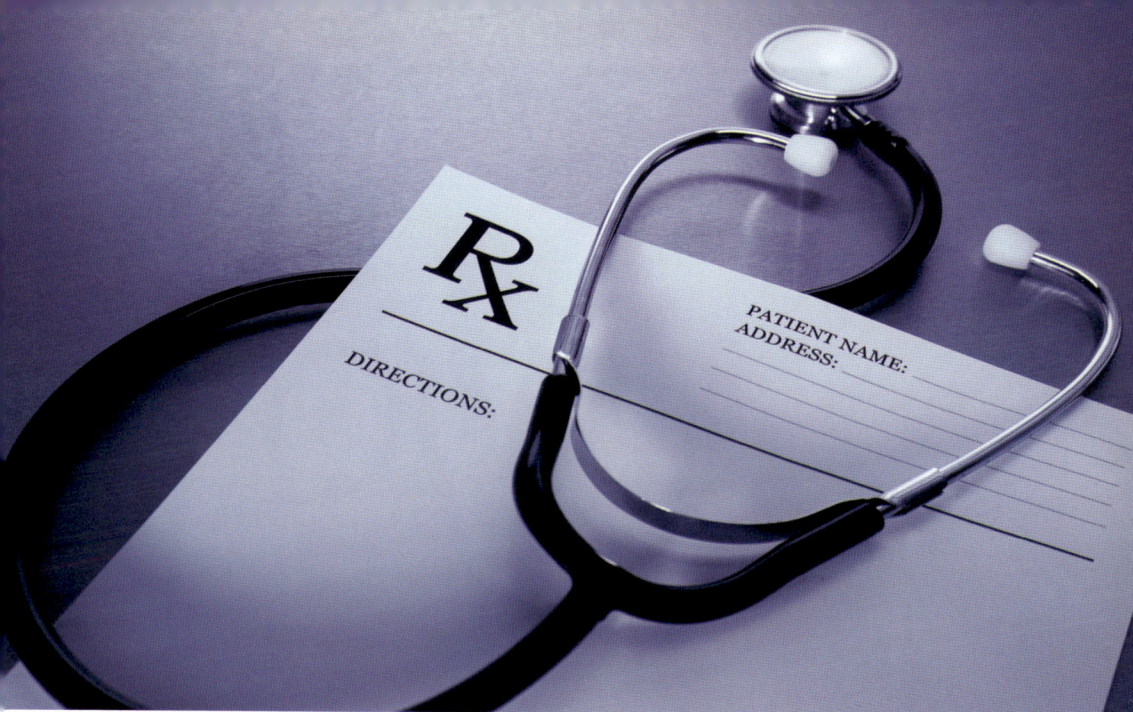

A medical practitioner may prescribe Adderall® to treat ADHD.

ADHD

Methylphenidate (Ritalin), used often in the treatment of ADHD, is a central nervous system stimulant (CNSS) that may block the reuptake of dopamine into presynaptic neurons. Researchers are not yet certain of exactly how methylphenidate works to increase attention, but it has been assumed for some time that the drug stimulates the brain stem and the cortex, and recent studies appear to corroborate this theory. It may seem paradoxical that medications known for stimulating can also calm people. Researchers think, however, that in people with ADHD, stimulants such as methylphenidate achieve their positive effect by improving concentration, which in turn tones down the impulsivity and distractibility of the disorder.

paradoxical: Seemingly contradictory, inconsistent, unbelievable.

Doctors have no magic cures for intellectual disabilities.

Another stimulant used frequently in treatment of ADHD is Adderall, a combination of amphetamine and dextroamphetamine. Dextroamphetamine is sometimes used alone, as Dexedrine, and also in combination with amphetamine. These two drugs are like mirror images of each other, and some patients benefit from a combination of the two drugs. Adderall works by releasing dopamine and norepinephrine from presynaptic neurons. It also causes the release of serotonin when used at high doses.

Other classes of medications commonly used in treatment of ADHD include antidepressants, antihypertensives, and antipsychotics.

Intellectual Disabilities

While the low IQ associated with intellectual disabilities is not in itself treatable with psychiatric medications, disruptive behaviors sometimes found in patients with intellectual disabilities can often be controlled through medication. Aggression, self-injurious behaviors, and stereotypy are the three behaviors related to intellectual disabilities that are most commonly treated with psychiatric drugs.

Neuroleptics, also called antipsychotics, are the drugs commonly used to control self-injurious and aggressive behaviors. Standard antipsychotics block the neurotransmitter dopamine and usually begin to work within a few days. Atypical antipsychotics have far fewer side effects than standard antipsychotics.

Assessing the Effects of Medication

In his book *The New Psychiatry*, Dr. Jack M. Gorman stresses the importance of a patient's knowing whether or not the prescribed medication is working. "The one advantage of medication over other forms of psychiatric treatment is that an effect is usually discernible in a matter of weeks; no one should ever continue to take medication unless it is clear there is a benefit," he says. In order to assess this, he encourages patients to realize that psychiatric drugs cannot: improve one's basic personality, give one job success or a better marriage, make one smarter, more athletic, or a better parent. Instead, their effect—usually quite concrete—is to relieve and often eliminate specific symptoms that may interfere with a person's social, home, professional, or academic life. The relief of these symptoms often allows the individual a better chance of improving other areas of life as well.

Drugs do not always either work or fail; they can also work partially, in which case they would reduce target symptoms but not eliminate them. If this happens, the medical practitioner and patient face the decision of whether or not to raise the dose, add a second drug to augment the first, change drugs, or turn to psychotherapy without drugs. The practitioner will continuously weigh the

Head banging and body rocking are the two most common stereotypic behaviors. Children apparently engage in these behaviors as a form of self-stimulation, whether to soothe themselves or to discharge tension. Up to half of all normal children exhibit this behavior at one time or another, engaging in thumb sucking, body rocking, nail biting, or similar behaviors. The incidence is much higher in deaf and blind children and in children with intellectual disabilities, pervasive developmental disorders, or psychotic disorders. Among individuals who have severe intellectual disabilities, the incidence of this disorder is as high as 60 percent. Head banging and body rocking may begin as early as six to twelve months of age. In normal children, however, these behaviors will typically disappear by the time the child is four years old. When the behavior does not resolve by itself, treatment includes behavior modification techniques, medication, and providing the child with alternatives to these self-stimulating behaviors.

Stereotypic movements may include:

- head banging
- body rocking
- hand flapping
- whirling
- stereotypic laughter
- thumb sucking
- hair fingering
- facial touching
- eye poking
- object biting
- self-biting
- self-scratching
- self-hitting
- teeth grinding
- holding breath

risks, benefits, and side effects of medication to determine the right direction to take for each patient.

Although drug therapy does not provide a simple solution to most of the disorders discussed in this book, drug treatment does provide concrete help—and real hope—to the thousands of children and their parents who experience these disorders. In some disorders, medication can relieve symptoms competely, and the patient may not need to seek additional therapy. In other more complex disorders, the medication may relieve the symptoms enough so the person can then work through painful issues in psychotherapy—and these issues may have contributed to the disorder in the first place. Each individual is different and needs to be evaluated by a qualified practitioner to determine the best course of treatment.

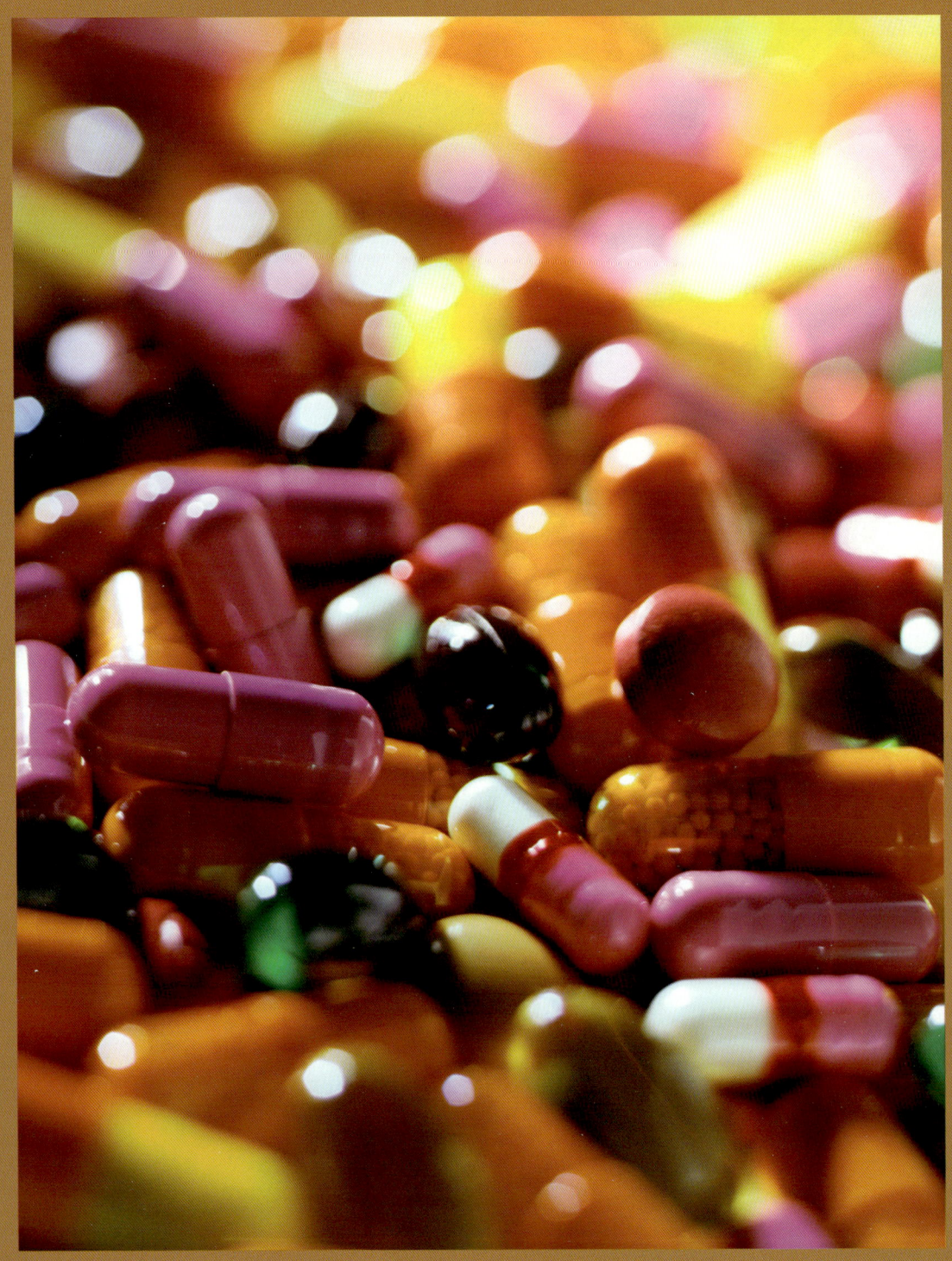
Psychiatric drugs may be a part of the treatment plan for a disorder first diagnosed in childhood or adolescence.

Chapter Four

Treatment Descriptions

Treatment for the disorders first diagnosed during adolescence and childhood vary from disorder to disorder. Even for the same disorder, treatment programs differ from individual to individual. No two people are exactly alike, and therapy must be adapted to the unique needs of each child.

Finding out about others who experience the same disorder helps someone with Tourette's disorder feel less frightened and alone.

Tourette's Disorder

Troy found that reading about Tourette's, as Dr. Johnson recommended, helped him understand much more about the strange disorder he'd had for so many years. He read about:

- a fifteen-year-old girl who became unconscious for several days after a fall from a horse, and when she awoke, began to experience symptoms of Tourette's.
- a Zulu healer from South Africa who called Tourette's one of the seven diseases considered sacred by his people and said that people with Tourette's (called Indiki by his people) were either made into chiefs, kings, or healers.
- several famous people who had Tourette's, including classical flutist and conductor Paige Vickery and Chris Jackson (Mahmoud Abdul-Rauf), a professional basketball player formerly with the Denver Nuggets.

tardive dyskinesia: A disorder of rhythmical, involuntary muscle movements, sometimes irreversible.

Troy began to understand that many people had to deal with the same problems he was facing and that many were doing so successfully. He felt a sense of kinship with other people who had Tourette's. He also felt less alone than he had since second grade, because both of his parents read the same articles and books he did, then discussed them with him.

At the same time, Dr. Johnson began treating Troy with a drug that would allow him to control his tics, though it might not completely stop them. "The most effective drugs we have for this are Haldol and Orap, both antipsychotics," the doctor told Troy and his parents. "They are thought to work by decreasing dopamine transmission to the basal ganglia. The problem is, they may increase your risk of **tardive dyskinesia**, which causes uncontrolled movements in the mouth and lips. So we'll start with one of the newer, atypical antipsychotics called risperidone (Risperdal), which has fewer side effects. You're the same weight as an adult, so we can go with the adult dosage, starting out with 1 milligram and increasing it by another milligram, on the second day and third day. Your ultimate dose will be between 4 and 8 milligrams."

Troy noticed little in the way of side effects from the risperidone, except a slight feeling of light-headedness and some sporadic headaches. Over a period of several months, he noticed a lessening of the strong compulsion to perform the tics. He gained the ability to control his behavior without a buildup of the tension he had previously experienced when suppressing the tics. With the combination of risperidone and educating himself about Tourette's, Troy began to come out of his shell, little by little. Within a few weeks, he began to show signs of the friendly, outgoing personality he had once had. As his behavior stabilized and he stopped fearing the sudden urges to perform his tics, Troy began feeling more comfortable around other students at high school. Within the year, he began making friends and entered more into the social life of the school. He eventually got a part in South Pacific, the musical his high school was performing.

Other Drugs Used to Treat Tic Disorders

- Ziprasidone (an atypical antipsychotic). The FDA warns that this drug could cause heart failure and death in elderly patients.
- Clonodine a centrally acting alpha-agonist.
- Guanfacine, another centrally acting alpha-agonist.
- Haloperidol, a standard antipsychotic.
- Pimozide, a standard antipsychotic.
- Imipramine hydrochloride, a TCA.
- Nortriptyline hydrochloride, a TCA.
- Clonazepam, a benzodiazepine.

Pervasive Developmental Disorders

Mary and Jay Janoski met regularly over the next several years with the doctor who had diagnosed Tracy's autistic disorder. They reported changes in Tracy's symptoms, such as a marked increase in violent temper tantrums when her routine was altered and her new habit of biting at her hands when she was upset by loud noises.

The doctor helped them understand that there is currently no drug available that can "cure" autism, but that drugs can be used as valuable adjunct therapy, to help reduce maladaptive behaviors that interfere with

adjunct: Something added to another thing, but that is not really a part of it.

maladaptive: Making it harder to get along in the real world.

Children with autism benefit from an appropriate educational program.

The FDA bases its approval on specific research results. Sometimes, a particular use for a drug may have been thoroughly researched by many studies, while other uses lack the same amount of research. In that case, the drug label will only include the uses that have met the FDA's stringent research requirements. Physicians, however, may continue to prescribe that drug for other "off-label" uses.

learning and other treatments. Such behaviors would include Tracy's temper tantrums and self-abusive behaviors; in other children these behaviors might include severe hyperactivity, aggression, irritability, social withdrawal, and other repetitive behaviors. He encouraged the Janoskis to enroll Tracy in a therapy program for children with autistic disorder at the local hospital. "The earlier, the better," he told them. "The evidence indicates that early intervention actually influences the way the brain develops."

"But how could we ever put her into a therapy program with these violent behaviors?" Jay asked.

"That's where the medications come in," the doctor answered. "We can start Tracy on a drug that can help control these self-destructive and aggressive behaviors, then do behavioral therapy in conjunction with the medicine. We should start now and continue therapy through Tracy's teenage years in order to give her the best chance possible to learn to function with autism."

Tracy responded well to small doses of fluvoxamine (Luvox), although this drug is not yet approved by the FDA for children under the age of eighteen. Her self-destructive behavior and her anger were both brought under control enough to allow her to be enrolled in the therapy program, where she received training in speech and language development, listening, vision, and music. Slowly, over the course of several years, Tracy learned to talk and began to interact with her parents and teachers.

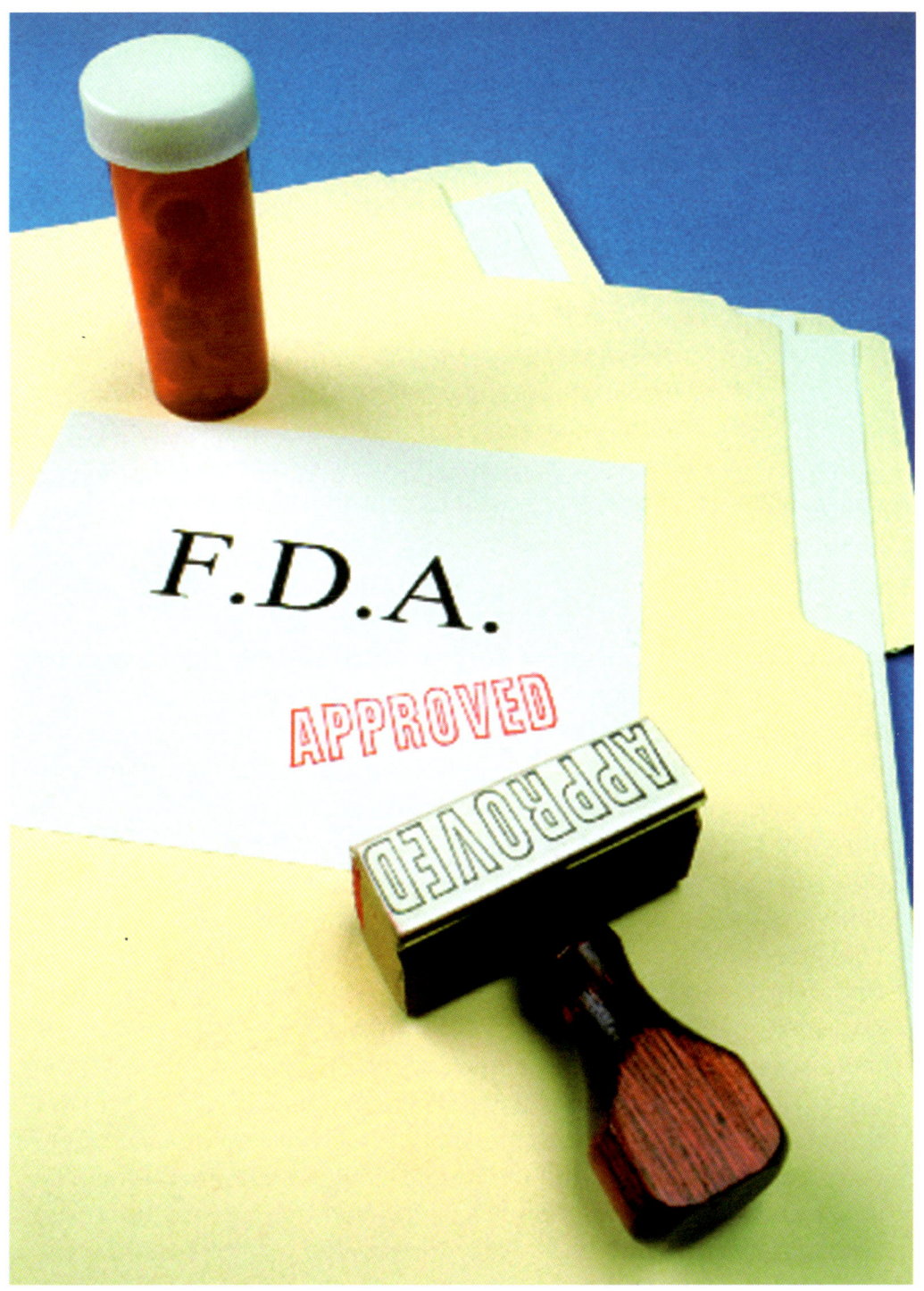

The FDA has high standards for the drugs it approves.

Other Drugs Used to Treat Pervasive Developmental Disorders

Because there is no known treatment for this disorder, only the symptoms can be treated. For the most part, these include drugs with primary effects on the dopamine and serotonin systems. Risperidone is an atypical antipsychotic. Research indicates that risperidone may help symptoms of aggression in youths with autistic disorder and other pervasive developmental disorders. Beta-blockers, clonidine, benzodiazepines, lithium, anticonvulsants, other antipsychotics, and naltrexone are also used to treat symptoms of aggression and self-abuse. SSRIs and anfranil are used to control repetitive behaviors.

ADD/ADHD

When Danny was diagnosed with ADHD, the doctor prescribed Ritalin, but explained that it had to be taken at intervals throughout the day, since the effectiveness of each dose lasted only a certain number of hours. Carrie had reservations about having Danny take Ritalin during the school day. She could see a huge difference in his ability to concentrate within a short time after he took his morning dose, and she was convinced that he truly benefited from the medication. But what would the other kindergartners think if he had to take more medicine at lunchtime? Would they tease him? Or worse, treat him as though he were different?

When the doctor heard Carrie's concern, he was able to set her mind at ease by prescribing a new way to take Ritalin—through the use of a twenty-four-hour MPH patch (MethyPatch). He could have prescribed other once-a-day medications as well—for instance, Concerta and Adderall XR both last ten to twelve hours, and Ritalin LA and Focalin last eight to nine hours; the FDA has recently approved Strattera, yet another once-a-day medication for the treatment of ADD/ADHD. Once this detail was taken care of, Danny's behavior at his full-day kindergarten class evened out. He was able to control himself much more effectively, sit still, and be attentive for longer periods of time than ever.

Danny's doctor also made clear to Carrie that Ritalin was only part of the treatment Danny needed. A complete treatment program for children with ADHD includes psychological, social, and educational therapies, as well as drug treatment. The medication would control Danny's ADHD symptoms, but many children like Danny also have problems with low self-esteem, poor social skills, family problems, and academic difficulties. Each child with ADHD will have specific needs; a doctor, psychiatrist, or psychologist can help the family determine which services are appropriate.

Other Drugs Used to Treat ADHD

Adderall, a combination of dextroamphetamine sulfate and saccharate with amphetamine sulfate and aspartate, is now being used in ADHD treatment. Several clinical studies have established Adderall as a safe and efficient drug for this disorder. Dexidrine is also used to treat ADHD.

A new class of drugs called ampakines are being developed, which increase the efficiency of glutamate binding to the AMPA glutamate receptors, promoting an increased current flow. Ampakines increase attention span and concentration, and are still being evaluated for use in ADHD treatment.

Atomoxetine (Strattera) is also being studied in trials. This drug was designed especially for ADHD. As a noradrenergic reuptake inhibitor, atomoxetine increases norepinephrine levels, thus attacking the

---

glutamate: A chemical found in nerve cells.

noradrenergic reuptake inhibitor: A medication that interferes with the movement of norepinephrine (or noradrenaline) in the brain.

norepinephrine: A neurotransmitter found in the peripheral and central nervous systems. Also called noradrenaline.

problem of ADHD from a different direction. Wellbutrin and TCAs have also proved to have positive results.

Intellectual Disabilities

Kelly Davis showed slow but fairly steady progress when she was able to attend school consistently. However, her behavioral problems, which included periodically banging her head against walls, had to be dealt with in order to allow her to stay in school. At the joint meeting of Kelly's parents, teachers, counselor, and pediatrician, it was agreed that a small dose of the atypical antipsychotic risperidone would be prescribed. Because few dependable studies on the use of antipsychotics in children have been done, the pediatrician felt it was particularly important to use one of the newer, atypical antipsychotics, which have fewer side effects. The entire team agreed that the drug would be used in conjunction with behavioral therapy and that Kelly's condition would be monitored closely by the pediatrician so that side effects would be picked up quickly.

Other Drugs Used to Treat Patients with Intellectual Disabilities

Neuroleptics are the most widely used psychiatric drugs for treating destructive, self-injurious, and stereotypic behaviors and aggression. Opiate receptor antagonists (also known as opioid blockers) such as naltrexone hydrochloride (ReVia, Trexane) have in some cases been shown to be useful in treating self-injurious behaviors, such as self-biting. However, in other cases, self-injurious behaviors appear to initially be made worse by opiate blockers. According to a study in the December 1999 issue of the *Journal of the American Academy of Child and Adolescent Psychiatry*, more than thirty adults with intellectual disabilities and self-injurious behaviors had no positive effects from the use of naltrexone.

> **neuroleptics:** Antipsychotic drugs.

HCFA Guidelines for Psychotropic Drug Use with Patients Who Have Mental Retardation

The Health Care Financing Administration (HCFA) has established guidelines for the use of psychotropic drugs in patients with intellectual disabilities. The following information is adapted from these guidelines:

- Before medication can be prescribed for a person with intellectual disabilities, other causes (such as medical or environmental) for the behavioral problem must be ruled out.
- The "least intrusive and most positive interventions" must be used, which may include behavior therapy and psychotherapy. In some cases, medication may be the least intrusive and most positive intervention.
- Medication should not be used as the sole treatment, but as part of a complete treatment program designed for the particular individual.
- Medication used should not make the patient less functional.
- The lowest dose of medication possible, but effective, should be used.
- A gradual reduction of the medication dose should be considered at least every year.

Even worse, naltrexone appeared to make the stereotypic behaviors worse in some of the patients studied.

Drugs that block the reuptake of serotonin are now being studied for use in moderating aggression, stereotypies, self-injurious behaviors, and compulsive behaviors, all of which are found at times in

Drug Holidays

"Drug holidays" are sometimes recommended for children on medication. Recent research, however, indicates that taking weekends off their medication is often not the best plans for children and adolescents with ADHD.

The child's symptoms not only impair his academic life but all aspects of life, and he will need his medication in order to function well at home as well as in school. For example, those individuals who have the inattentive subtype of ADHD need to consider the demands they face on the weekend. If they don't need to pay attention to anything in particular, then they may be able to go without their medication. However, what if the adolescent is driving on the weekend? Inattention and distractibility could be dangerous, even life-threatening, if the individual is behind the wheel, operating machinery, or even riding a bike through heavy traffic.

One reason for "drug holidays" is that parents are sometimes concerned because children often lose weight when taking medication for ADHD, since the drug may suppress their appetites. If a child experiences significant weight loss, there are a few options:

- change the medication to another type
- add another drug (like Remeron) that will increase appetite as well as improve sleep
- give higher calorie foods and more frequent small meals

conjunction with intellectual disabilities. Clomipramine hydrochloride (Anafranil), a TCA, has proven effective in treating repetitive behaviors in children with autism and people who have intellectual disabilities.

When using psychiatric drugs to treat children and adolescents, doctors, psychiatrists, and advanced practice nurses, must take into account that young people's bodies and brains are not yet fully formed and may react differently to psychiatric drugs than do the bodies and brains of adults. Practitioners who specialize in the mental disorders of childhood and adolescence are important sources of information on this subject and should be included in treatment decisions.

School may present many challenges to a child with ADHD.

Chapter Five

Case Studies

Each individual who experiences disorders first diagnosed in childhood is unique. But they all have some things in common, as well, and many of them find that drug therapy helps them handle their symptoms.

ADHD

For Tony, school was trouble from the very beginning. Even though his birthday just missed the cutoff date for kindergarten, so he had nearly another year to mature further before he started his school career, Tony managed to get into daily trouble with his kindergarten teacher. He jumped out of his seat many times each day; he was restless and fidgety; he made life miserable for the children who sat near him by grabbing their crayons and markers out of their hands. No matter how many times he was sent to the office to meet with the principal, Tony still called other students inappropriate names and frequently yelled out during story and rest times.

Tony had never met his father. His mother worked two jobs, and although she loved her son dearly, she could rarely be around to parent Tony, who was supervised for the most part by an aunt and uncle who lived in the next-door apartment and had seven children of their own. While Tony was in kindergarten and the early elementary grades, the constant news that he had gotten in trouble at school yet again made little impact at home and at his relatives'. Everyone was just too busy to pay much attention.

By the time he reached the fourth grade, Tony was a social outcast. His impulsive, disruptive behavior annoyed and angered his mother, his aunt, uncle, and cousins, and the students and teachers at his school. The other fourth graders considered him to be immature and "strange." Because he did not follow the rules in any game, he was always shunned at recess and chosen last for teams in physical education.

In the fifth grade, Tony was approached by two eighth-grade boys who lived in his neighborhood. For two days, they let him "hang" with them, showing him how to shoot baskets and buying him french fries at the local fast-food restaurant. When they offered him cocaine, Tony had the feeling he was making a wrong decision, but their friendship was worth it. It was the only friendship he'd ever experienced.

By the tenth grade, Tony was both an alcoholic and a drug addict. He'd been arrested several times and was getting into street fights regularly. Tony missed school more days than he attended, and he dropped out for good on the day he turned sixteen.

Then two things happened that turned his life around. First, his mother lost her waitressing job but then found a new one doing laundry at the local homeless shelter. Though it paid no better than her old job, she got to know the shelter director, who had worked with many troubled young people. Second, shortly after his mother began working at the homeless shelter, Tony nearly died from a drug overdose.

Tony's mother was determined to stay at the hospital with him until he was out of the critical stage. She had to explain to the director of the homeless shelter, Mr. Reems, why she was taking a day off work, and in doing so, she communicated her distress about Tony's problems in school and about her struggles to take care of him. Mr. Reems was touched by her deep concern for her son, and he decided to look into Tony's case.

After talking with Tony's teachers, his mother, and Tony himself, Mr. Reems realized that although Tony had never been diagnosed, he had ADHD. Mr. Reems explained to Tony's mother and to Tony that he believed an early diagnosis of ADHD, with appropriate intervention, could have averted much of the tragedy in Tony's life. Now, however, there were other layers of problems on top of the ADHD: the alcohol and drug addiction, the social alienation, and an obviously destructive lifestyle that included poor nutrition.

"Your problems won't be a simple thing to solve, Tony," Mr. Reems said.

Tony, still lying in bed at the hospital, shrugged and nodded. Even though he didn't understand exactly what his problems were, he knew they weren't simple. Deep inside, he wanted more than anything to live the kind of life he saw so many other people living—a life of satisfying relationships, pursuing goals and dreams, and making a decent living. But all that was beyond him. He didn't know why; he just knew that he always messed up everything. He was a loser, that was all.

Mr. Reems had seen the same self-condemning attitude in other teenagers he had worked with, and he recognized it now as he talked further with Tony. For the next half hour, Mr. Reems explained to Tony and his mother about a school he knew—an alternative school—for kids in the same or similar situations to Tony's. The

Young men with untreated ADHD are more apt to get in trouble with the law.

Criminal Activity and ADHD in Young Men

ADHD can have long-term effects if not treated properly. Effects can last through adolescent years into adulthood. They include:

- Poor academic performance: Children with ADHD are eventually more likely to complete less school (2–3 years on average), achieve lower grades, and perform poorly on standardized tests.
- Poor social functioning: Untreated ADHD can lead to fewer friends, along with lower self-esteem and social skills.
- Criminality: People, especially boys, with ADHD are more likely to have a record of criminal activity, including higher rates of arrests, convictions, and time spent in prison.

school was in the country, two hundred miles away, and Tony would have to go and agree to stay for at least a year. "But they know how to deal with the things you're facing," Mr. Reems said. "They do it all the time. It's not an easy program, but if you really want to get clean and then work on your other problems, the faculty at this school can show you the way."

Tony's mother glanced at her hands, clenched together in her lap, and began to cry. "Probably only rich kids can go there—" she began.

Mr. Reems stopped her. "I've referred kids to this school for years, and the majority of them had very little money. There's a scholarship program, donated mostly by families of kids who have gone there and turned their lives around. And now, some of the kids who went on to do well are donating, too. If Tony really wants to change, I'll do everything I can to get him admitted."

Tony's mother looked at her son, waiting for an answer. It seemed like a dream to Tony, a place where someone would help him. It was also frightening, thinking of what it could mean to go off the drugs and the alcohol. He looked around the hospital room and felt the pinch of the IV in his arm. He knew he never wanted to be in this situation again. He nodded at his mother and Mr. Reems. "Okay."

A month later, Tony was strong enough to leave for the school. The first weeks were terrible as he continued to struggle through withdrawal, but he made it. He became involved with Alcoholics Anonymous (AA), where mentors supported and helped guide him toward a life of sobriety. Before he actually began classes at the school, Tony was given several days of academic and psychological testing. He was officially diagnosed with ADHD, and Wellbutrin was prescribed. This drug also decreases cravings for other chemical substances. Tony set about changing lifelong habits with the help of behavioral therapy.

> mentors: Counselors or guides.

A Beneficial Side Effect

Research by Biederman and Wilen indicates that treating ADHD with stimulants actually decreases the risk of alcohol and substance use disorders—while adolescents with ADHD who are left untreated have much higher rates of:

- substance abuse
- car accidents
- school failure
- speeding tickets

Tony struggled tremendously during his three years at the school, but he was committed to achieving the kind of life he wanted so much. When he finally graduated, he was drug and alcohol free, and he felt he had developed the inner strength necessary to maintain that lifestyle. He had learned ways to focus and direct his attention when he studied, and he was accepted into a technical school that would train him for a career.

Tourette's Disorder

Carissa was smart and talented—everyone recognized that. By the time she was nine, she could play some Beethoven sonatas and Chopin compositions better than her piano teacher. She was always on the honor roll at her school, and her teachers depended on her to be responsible and well behaved. Carissa's parents congratulated themselves on raising such a fine child, and they couldn't help but feel that their daughter's successes reflected well on them.

Then they got a phone call from the head counselor at Carissa's summer camp. At first, they couldn't believe what they were hearing. Carissa was making snorting and grunting sounds and refused to stop. "Not only that," the head counselor said, "but she's repeating the last few words everyone else is saying, and the other campers are getting very annoyed with her."

The phone call made no sense to Carissa's parents. In fact, they thought at first that it was a joke, but then they asked to speak to Carissa and heard her sobbing on the other end of the phone line. They made the two-and-a-half-hour drive to the camp, where they found a shaken, red-eyed Carissa who did exactly what the counselor had reported, usually for several minutes at a time with periods of quiet in between.

After a long conversation with their daughter, they understood that Carissa had begun feeling strong urges to perform these behaviors several months before. "At first it was just stuff like blinking my eyes hard and shaking my head quick, like this." She showed her parents what she meant. "But I could hide that. I just did it when I was alone, or when no one was looking. But then I got here and all this other stuff started—" Carissa was unable to finish her sentence.

To avoid any further embarrassment for her, Carissa's parents helped her pack her things when the other campers were out of the cabin. They drove her home and got her settled back in her own room. Then they called their family doctor for a recommendation as to what they should do next. He got them in to see a psychiatrist the next day, one who was experienced in working with children with Tourette's disorder.

The psychiatrist was kind and patient, reassuring both Carissa and her parents that sometimes tics began this way, with little warning. Because Carissa's tics were so strong that they interfered with her normal life, the psychiatrist prescribed medication to help Carissa control them. After a long conversation with Carissa, the psychiatrist explained to the family that their daughter had been under a good deal of pressure at camp, where several of the other campers seemed to go out of their way to exclude her. "That pressure may have contributed to both the tics and the echolalia. The good news is that, very often, these tics die away on their own. We'll keep Carissa on the medication for six months or so, in order to help her get a good start in school in the fall, then start to wean her off it gradually. Meanwhile, I'll meet with her each week to help her learn ways to control the tics."

> **echolalia:** Repetition of overheard words or phrases.

By the time Carissa entered high school, she was only rarely experiencing the urge to perform the tics, and only when she was under great stress. She had taken the medication throughout the most difficult stage of her Tourette's, but because it helped her control the urge to perform the tics, only her family and closest friends knew about the problem.

There are no magic answers for the young people who experience these disorders. But drug treatment can help them live lives that are

Drug treatment combined with family support can bring hope to people like Carissa.

Case Studies • 95

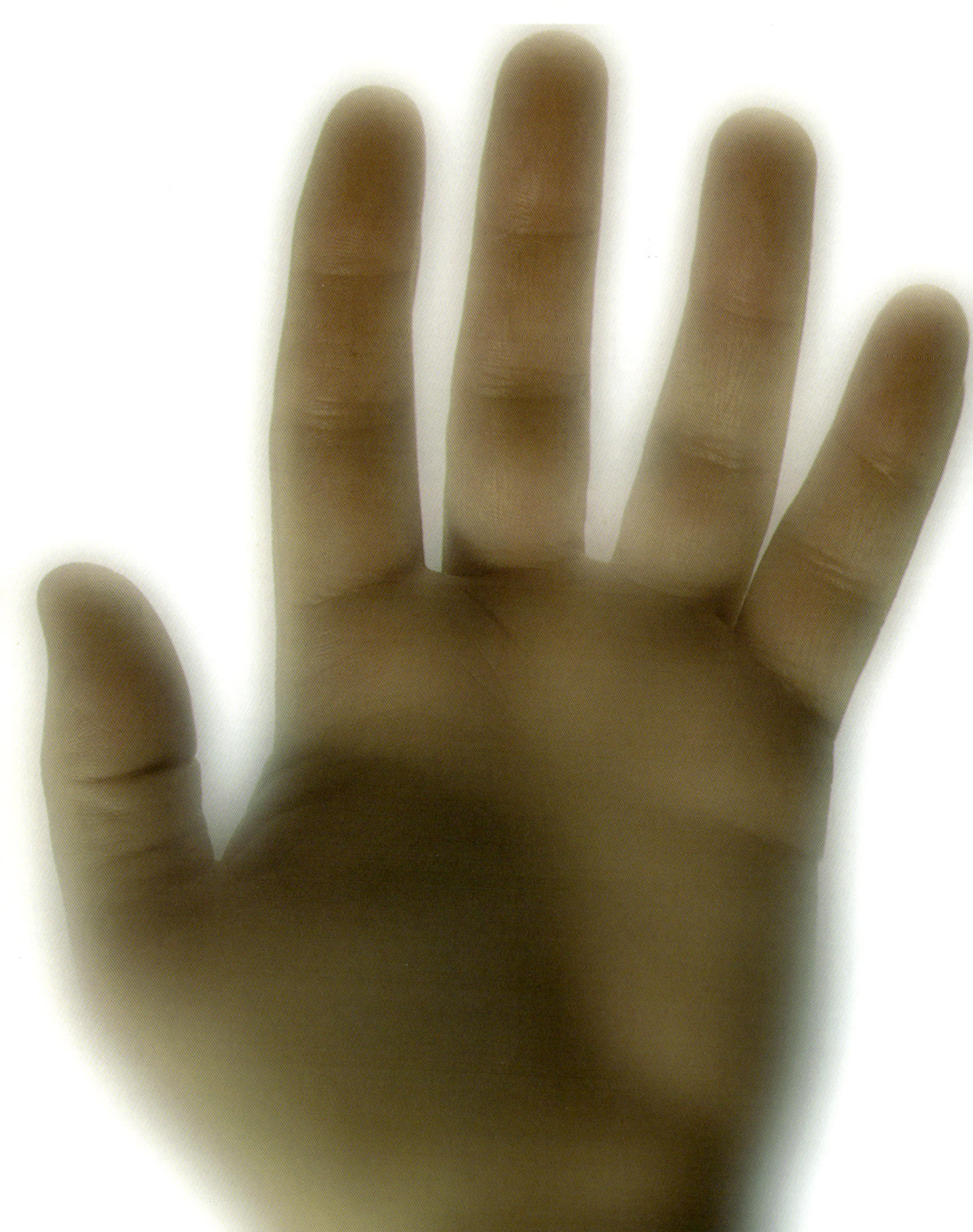

Tics may include uncontrollable hand motions.

more satisfying and productive. They will also need ongoing supplemental therapy (counseling and behavioral therapy, for instance). These various treatment programs give hope to the families and individuals who face the disorders diagnosed in childhood and adolescence.

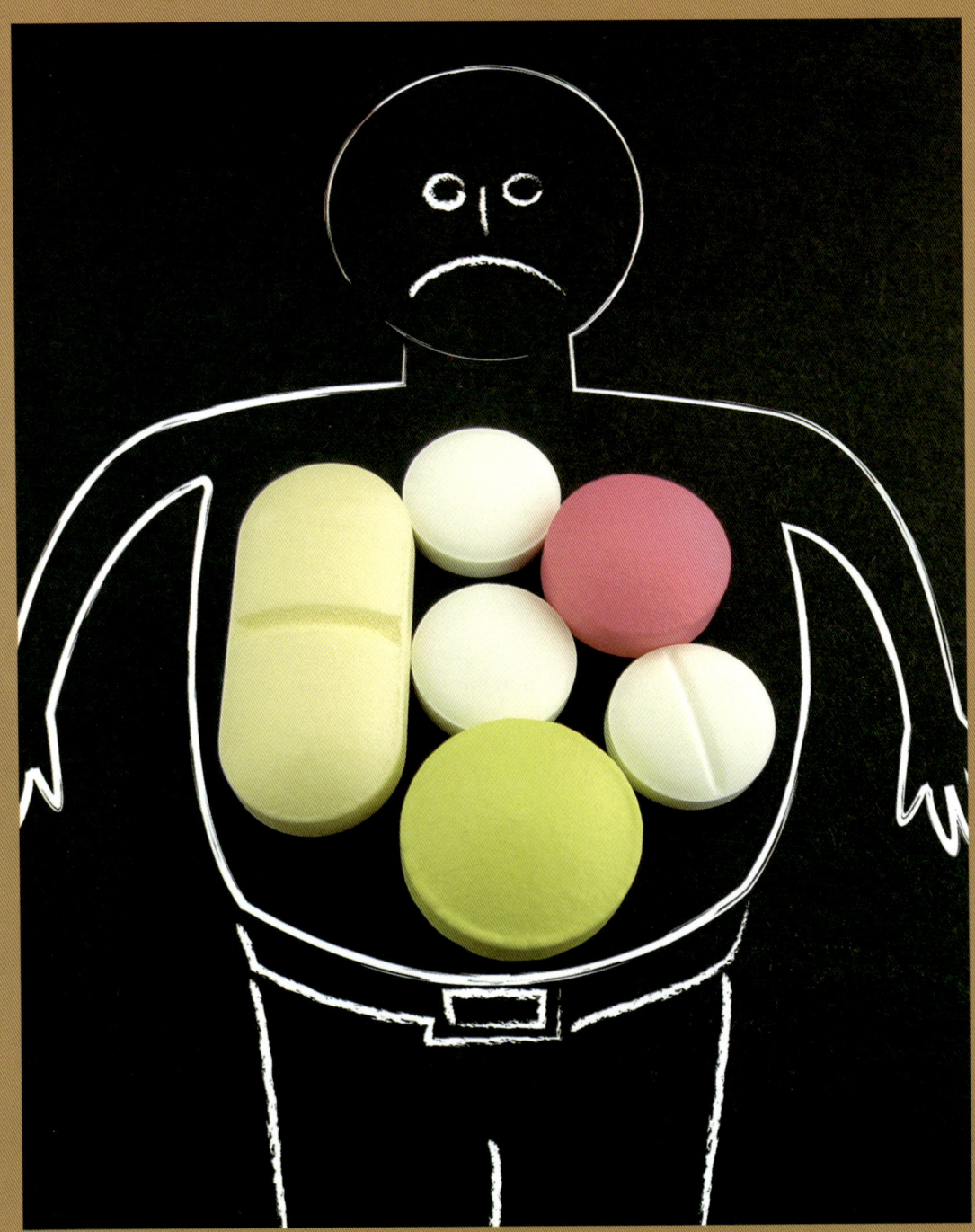

Drug treatment is not a magic cure. Drugs are powerful substances that can also have unwanted side effects.

Chapter Six

Risks and Side Effects

In his book *The New Psychiatry*, Jack Gorman, M.D., gives a simple summary of what a drug side effect is—"anything a drug does that we don't want it to do"—and explains that any chemical substance we put into out bodies affects more than just the one part of our body we want it to affect. He likens this to the food we eat, using a steak as an example of a good source of needed protein for our bodies. He then points out that steak can do other things to our bodies, including increasing our cholesterol level and adding unwanted weight. Some people will consider both these positive and negative effects of eating steak, and decide to go ahead and eat the steak; for them, the benefits outweigh the risks. In much the same way, drugs can provide needed benefits but also produce unwanted side effects, although some may be much more serious than the "side effects" of eating steak. In some cases, the benefits will outweigh the side effects to the degree that many people will decide they will take the drugs and find ways to deal with the side effects.

Following are the main classes of drugs used to treat these disorders, with possible side effects:

Antipsychotics

Standard Side Effects
- emotional blunting
- fatigue
- weight gain
- sexual dysfunction
- dry mouth
- muscular (includes decreased muscle movements, rigidity, tremor, muscle spasms, restlessness)
- tardive dyskinesia (abnormal, involuntary, constant, rhythmical muscle movements)

Atypical Side Effects
- sedation
- restlessness
- Clozapine can cause agranulocytosis, in which the body quits producing white blood cells, and can lead to infection and even death.

According to Dr. Edward Drummond, all antipsychotics have the potential to cause neuroleptic malignant syndrome, a "rare but severe and potentially fatal reaction consisting of fever, muscle rigidity, mental status changes, and alterations in pulse and blood pressure."

Benzodiazepines

- sedation
- poor physical coordination
- memory impairment

When used daily for months:

- dulled emotions
- impairment of cognitive skills
- contribute to depression
- addiction

All drugs should be used with caution. Otherwise, the treatment may be as dangerous as the disorder.

SSRIs can cause changes in sleep patterns.

Selective Serotonin Reuptake Inhibitors (SSRIs)

- changes in sleep patterns
- fatigue
- occasionally cause agitation
- decreased sexual drive/impaired sexual response
- gastrointestinal distress
- dizziness

Tricyclic Antidepressants (TCAs)

- weight gain
- dry mouth
- constipation
- sweating
- light-headedness due to low blood pressure

Monoamine Oxidase Inhibitors (MAOIs)

- weight gain
- dry mouth
- insomnia
- impaired sexual response
- light-headedness due to low blood pressure
- potential to cause a stroke if taken with adrenaline or adrenaline-like substances (found in cough/cold medicines; food products such as aged cheese, processed meats)

Always follow your doctor's and pharmacist's instructions when taking any drug.

Special Circumstances

Children and adolescents with intellectual disabilities may react differently to standard psychiatric drugs than do average children. The adage "start low, go slow" is considered especially important with individuals with intellectual disabilities. Those with Down syndrome may be far more sensitive than usual to the anticholinergic drugs (these are drugs that actively inhibit the cholinergic nervous system); some may react with more sensitivity to effects of sedative-hypnotic drugs.

Medication must be integrated as part of a comprehensive treatment plan, which includes a behavior plan, communication between the prescribing doctor and other therapists, and the collection of behavioral data.

Stimulants

Stimulants have few side effects. However, on rare occasions, these drugs can:
- cause mild loss of appetite
- worsen existing tics or cause new ones
- worsen or cause psychotic thinking and manic episodes
- cause seizures (but this risk is very minimal)

Any medication people put into their bodies is capable of producing side effects. Many have risk factors. The best way for individuals to protect their health is to educate themselves about all possible side effects and to communicate regularly with their doctor.

A mother doses her child with alternative "natural" medicine. Such treatment is contoversial in today's world of psychiatric medicine.

Chapter Seven

Alternative and Supplementary Treatments

Drug treatment is certainly not the only solution to some of the disorders first diagnosed during childhood or adolescence. Other therapy can supplement—or offer an alternative to—medication.

Tourette's Disorder

One of the most important components in a treatment plan for a child or adolescent with Tourette's is the education of the patient and of those around him. Family members and teachers need to understand as much as possible about this disorder. Education can include reading material available from national support groups and

Some parents believe that a healthy natural diet helps their children with autism.

organizations such as the National Organization for Rare Disorders, Inc. (NORD) in Danbury, Connecticut (see the "For More Information" section at the back of this book). Educated families, teachers, and physicians can then advocate for the best school environment possible for the patient.

Autism

Along with her fluvoxamine treatment, Tracy also received intensive early intervention in motor and psychological areas as well as behavioral therapy. Techniques used by the therapists included food and other rewards (positive reinforcement) to help Tracy learn and use language. Another area the therapists focused on was that of social skills. In this area, also, therapists used structured, skill-oriented, individual instruction, as well as rewards, to help Tracy learn to relate to other humans, including children in the program and adults such as her own parents and her teachers.

Many researchers are very interested in discovering alternative treatments for autistic disorder. Because the cause of this disorder is not yet completely understood, many different foods, vitamins, and other substances are being tried on a trial-and-error basis. Alternatives currently being advocated for autistic disorder include the following treatments.

Dimethylglycine (DMG)

DMG is a compound that is classified as a food and sold in health food stores. There are claims that it helps improve speech in children with autism, usually within a week.

Special Diet

Some people have found that their child with autistic disorder improves when she is put on a diet that includes the following elements:

Vitamins may improve the functioning of children with autism. Not all reserachers agree, however, that vitamin therapy is beneficial.

Homeopathic Treatment for ADHD

Homeopathy is a form of alternative medicine that treats disease and disorders from a very different perspective than conventional medicine. It looks at a person's entire physical and mental being, rather than dividing a patient into various symptoms and disorders. Homeopathic medicine uses tiny doses to stimulate the body's ability to heal itself. In some cases, these doses may be administered only once every few months or years.

According to Judyth Reichenberg-Ullman and Robert Ullman, authors of *Ritalin Free Kids: Safe and Effective Homeopathic Medicine for ADHD and Other Behavioral and Learning Problems*, homeopathy offers safe, natural alternatives that can supplement or replace conventional pharmaceutical treatment. They recommend this form of treatment because it has fewer side effects than drugs like Ritalin.

- the use of unrefined and varied foods that are free of artificial colors, flavors, additives, and naturally occurring salicylates (apple juice contains salicylates).
- the removal of all wheat and dairy products. Some researchers believe that wheat gluten and casein from dairy products chemically form an opiate that puts some children into autistic-like states.
- avoiding foods with yeast, mold, or sugar.
- using filtered water and natural household products.

Sensory integration therapy for children with autism involves guided physical activities.

Vitamins and Supplements

In some studies, vitamin B6 is said to improve eye contact and speech in children with autism; this vitamin is also thought to reduce tantrum behavior. Many doctors, however, feel that these studies were flawed and, therefore, undependable.

Other vitamins and minerals said to be helpful include vitamin A, calcium, and magnesium. Supplements recommended include:

- essential fatty acids (in evening primrose oil, cod liver oil, or flaxseed)
- amino acids, including tryptophan, secretin, and GABA, which help with digestion
- antifungals, such as nystatin and Diflucan, and acidolpholous, which are important to combat yeast overgrowth (particularly after the use of antibiotics).

A practitioner should consult carefully with parents to formulate the best treatment plan for each child with a psychiatric disorder.

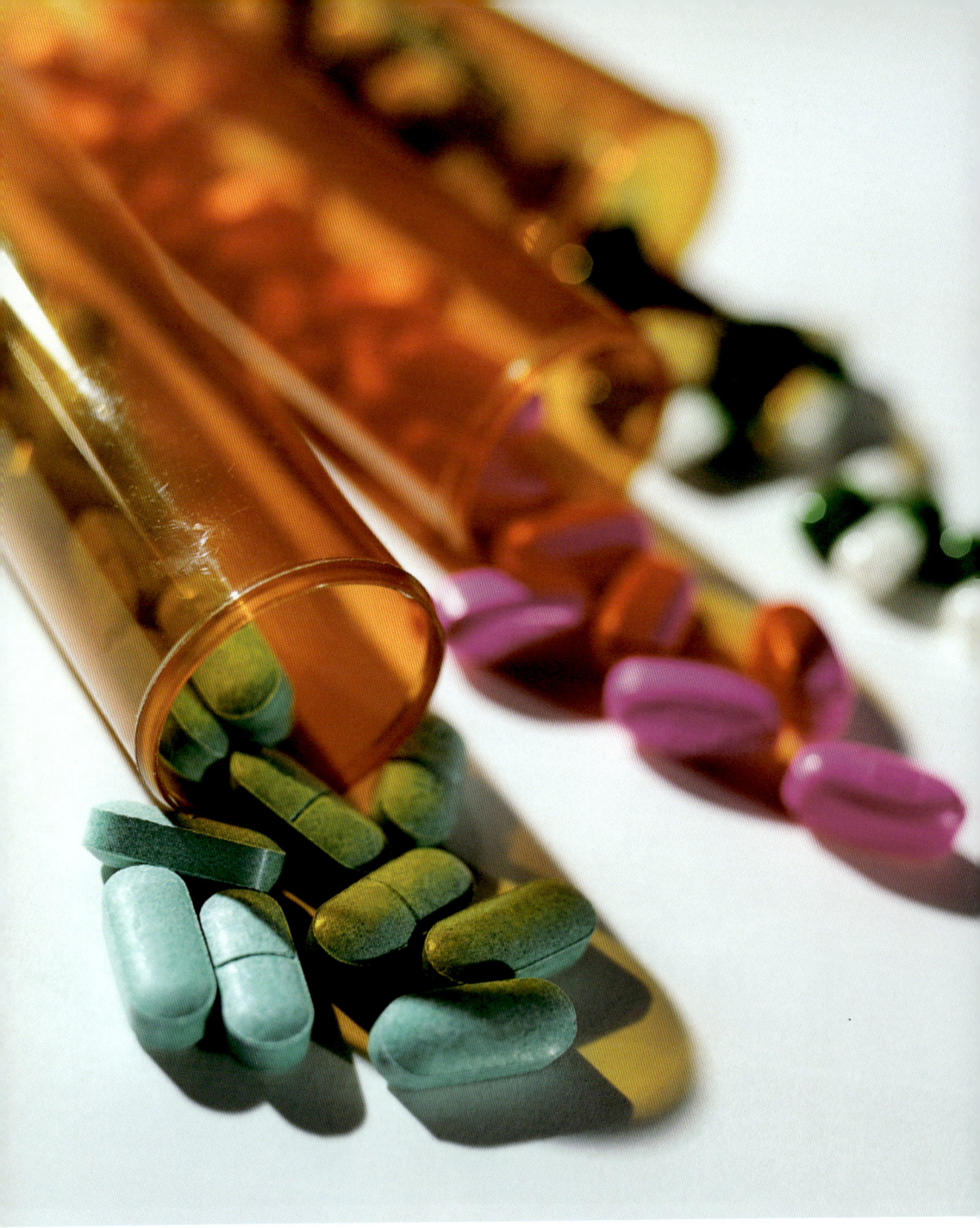

Not everyone agrees that ADHD should be treated with medication.

Therapies

- immunotherapy (therapy to combat what some believe to be vaccine-induced autism)
- sensory processing treatments (to help improve efficiency of processing information from the five senses; also addresses the problem of disturbed sense of balance due to repeated ear infections)
- sensory integration therapy (guided activities done by occupational or physical therapists that lead the body to make efficient and organized responses; facilitates appropriate responses to sensory input)
- auditory integration training (helps normalize the way sound is processed; stimulates balance, movement, and auditory systems)
- vision therapy (normalizes the way children with autism focus on and give meaning to what they see)
- structural therapies (restorative manipulative treatment to correct structural dysfunction caused by birth trauma)

Attention-Deficit and Disruptive Behavior Disorders

Few people who read or watch the media can miss the controversy that rages over whether or not to medicate children diagnosed with ADHD with the drug Ritalin. Richard DeGrandpre, in his book *Ritalin Nation*, explains that Ritalin is classified by the Drug Enforcement Administration (DEA) as a potent, potentially addictive substance. In the late 1960s, Ritalin was banned in Sweden after an epidemic of street abuse of this drug. However, Novartis (formerly Ciba Pharmaceuticals, and the manufacturer of this drug) calls Ritalin "a mild central nervous system stimulant." The *New York Times* describes it as a "mild stimulant" and compares it to a "jolt of strong coffee."

Children and Adults with Attention Deficit Disorders (CHADD) is the nation's largest ADHD support organization. CHADD was begun in 1987 by a small group of parents and professionals. Today, CHADD has grown to more than 16,000 members and 200 chapters nationwide. On the local level, CHADD sponsors parent support groups, convenes meetings featuring speakers, works with local school systems to ensure appropriate educational services for children with ADHD, and publishes local newsletters. The national office of CHADD provides information on the latest developments in ADHD-related issues.

There is also controversy over whether or not ADHD is a true diagnosis. One doctor, Peter R. Breggin, who is a psychiatrist and the founder of the International Center for the Study of Psychiatry and Psychology (ICSPP), says, "ADHD is a diagnosis that's false." Dr. Breggin thinks that all symptoms of ADHD actually indicate other problems that should be found and treated. Regarding the use of methylphenidate (Ritalin), Dr. Breggin says, "It crushes spontaneity, curiosity, and play." He is opposed to the use of medications to treat ADHD and is a primary consultant in a class action lawsuit against Novartis Pharmaceuticals, the American Psychiatric Association, and Children and Adults with Attention Deficit Disorder (CHADD). Many doctors, however, do believe that ADHD is a true diagnosis, and several are in favor of medicating children with ADHD symptoms when necessary.

In *Ritalin Nation*, Richard DeGrandpre states his idea that ADHD is not so much a brain dysfunction as it is evidence of human consciousness transformed by the rise of rapid-fire culture. DeGrandpre advocates nothing less than a complete restructuring of the way we—and our children—live our lives in order to produce a psychologically healthy environment in which children will not be addicted to overstimulation.

The following steps are adapted from DeGrandpre's list of ways to deal with what he sees as the underlying causes of ADHD:

> **paradigm**: A pattern, example, or model.

1. Break the sensory addiction that manifests itself in the symptoms we call ADD and ADHD. Create a slower pace of life. In time, this slower pace transforms human consciousness, and eventually transforms the children of our "rapid-fire" culture.
2. Challenge the "dominant **paradigm** of work, work, work." DeGrandpre advocates "redefining the bottom line" and purposely spending less time at work and more on parenting and teaching children effective life skills.
3. Return the senses to a natural speed and rhythm, through deliberate practice. Restrict yourself to a greater quality of experience instead of a greater quantity.
4. Return consciousness to real experience in real time. Instead of allowing children to become caught up in the simulated reality of television, films, and video games, give them hands-on experience of the real world.

Despite the ongoing controversy over drug treatment for ADHD, most scientific researchers today agree that medication is the best treatment option for children and adolescents with ADHD. Many children with ADHD who have not been treated will eventually have higher rates of:

- substance abuse
- academic and professional failure
- relationship problems
- legal problems

Alternative and Supplementary Treatments

Many experts in the medical field are skeptical of alternative treatments for ADHD. They believe that clinical practice should be based on findings from research studies not on opinion—and so far research has shown medication to be the only effective treatment for ADHD. Alternative treatments such as counseling for problems associated with ADHD (for instance, poor social skills or organizational skills) and support groups can be helpful—but they do not treat the core ADHD symptoms. However, many clinicians have different opinions on the subject.

5. Overcome cynicism through hope and action. DeGrandpre reminds readers that psychological problems are "often the embodiment of social problems," and that children who cannot cope with the stresses of modern life must not be labeled as ill. Instead, he encourages readers not to buy into the psychology that history is out of control and cannot be changed, a mind-set that undermines our capacity to live deliberately. DeGrandpre feels that society's acceptance of the fact that nearly 10 percent of our children exist on Ritalin—when only two decades ago the very idea caused outrage—is one sign of our culture's sense of hopelessness about the future.

In his book *Survival Strategies for Parenting Your ADD Child: Dealing with Obsessions, Compulsions, Depression, Explosive Behavior and Rage*, George T. Lynn calls children with ADD "attention different" children. (ADHD was formerly known as ADD, Attention Deficit Disorder.) He suggests that parents recognize the creative and intellectual abilities of their attention different children and says it is the "modern classroom, with its requirement for high volume rote learning that makes them appear deficit for they do not learn well in this setting." Lynn suggests using the "consultant model" of dealing with children with ADHD by being available to help but by also allowing the child to become more self-supporting and, thus, to need the parents' help less and less.

Research Results

A large study that compared treatment methods for ADHD found that medication alone and medication plus intensive behavioral therapy proved to be equal in effectiveness—and both were superior to behavioral treatment alone and community-based treatment.

Other studies indicate the toll taken on families where a child with ADHD is left untreated:

- parents often have to reduce their work hours
- parents may be forced to change jobs or stop working all together
- parents experience high levels of marital discord

Lynn details a number of specific ways to interact with an ADHD child that will allow him to express his motivation for his actions. He also advises parents to:

1. Give a child positive alternative choices, with encouragement to make the choices himself.
2. Move the child toward positive outcomes by using positive statements.
3. Manage transition times carefully, with many warnings ahead of time. Transitions from one activity to another can cause a child to feel "lost, out-of-control," anxious, and overwhelmed.

Lynn advocates a well-balanced diet with special vigilance for a "carbohydrate craving that may signal the presence of an addiction to refined carbs that many ADD children have and that can make behavior worse." He writes that physical exercise allows children to let off the pressure that "causes hyperactivity" and suggests encour-

Walter Jackson Bate

120 • Childhood & Adolescent Disorders

Walter Jackson Bate's Pulitzer Prize-winning biography, *Samuel Johnson*, includes the following excerpt about the human mind:

> . . . the mind—far from being either a serene, objective, rational instrument, or, as the radical materialist thought, a sort of recording machine that works in mechanically happy union with whatever outside experiences press the button—is something unpredictably alive in its own right. And when something outside stimulates or pokes it into activity, it can start moving in any number of unforeseen ways that are by no means in harmony with things outside it.

aging solo exercise because team sports may be difficult for children with this disorder.

It is not uncommon for people to "take sides" about the treatment of mental disorders, particularly in their children. Some advocate treatment with nothing but "natural" remedies, including compounds found in nature and vitamins. Others believe only psychotherapy and/or behavioral therapies should be used. Still others strongly favor the use of psychiatric drugs.

Because each of these categories may prove helpful in different circumstances, careful consideration of all options is necessary. Sometimes one treatment may be clearly indicated; at other times a combination of treatments may be necessary. For example, it may be necessary to intervene in a severe case of ADHD with temporary drug treatment and then follow up with the modification of a child's environment and greatly increased involvement on the part of her parents. Parents and other caregivers will want to educate themselves as much as possible and to give due consideration to each treatment option.

Further Reading

DeGrandpre, Richard, Ph.D. *Ritalin Nation: Rapid-Fire Culture and the Transformation of Human Consciousness*. New York: Norton, 2000.

Drummond, Edward. *The Complete Guide to Psychiatric Drugs*. New York: John Wiley & Sons, 2006.

Fowler, Mary. *Maybe You Know My Kid, A Parents' Guide to Identifying, Understanding and Helping Your Child with Attention-Deficit Hyperactivity Disorder*. New York: Citadel Press, 2000.

Friedberg, Robert D. and Jessica M. McClure. *Clinical Practice of Cognitive Therapy with Children and Adolescents*. New York: Guilford Press, 2002.

Gantos, Jack. *Joey Pigza Swallows the Key*. New York: Square Fish, 2011.

Gantos, Jack. *Joey Pigza Loses Control*. New York: Square Fish, 2011.

Gorman, Jack M. *The Essential Guide to Psychiatric Drugs*. New York: St. Martin's Griffin, 2007.

Park, Clara Claiborne. *Exiting Nirvana, A Daughter's Life with Autism*. Boston: Little, Brown, 2001.

Sacks, Oliver. *The Man Who Mistook His Wife for a Hat, and Other Clinical Tales*. New York: Simon and Schuster, 1985.

Stein, David B. *Ritalin Is Not the Answer*. San Francisco: Jossey-Bass, 2001.

Film

Twitch and Shout, an award-winning hour-long film that provides an intimate journey into the world of Tourette's syndrome. "What a wonderful, compassionate, funny, instructive, inspiring, and flat-out brilliant documentary. *Twitch and Shout* is likely to change your opinions, or change you, period. . . ." (*New York Daily News*)
For rental or purchase information about this film:

New Day Films
www.newday.com/index.html

For More Information

Autism Network International (ANI)
www.ani.ac

Autism Research Institute (ARI)
www.autismresearchinstitute.com

Children and Adults with Attention Deficit Disorder (CHADD)
www.chadd.org

Learning Disabilities Association of America
www.ldanatl.org

MAAP Services (for Autism, Asperger's Syndrome, and PDD)
www.maapservices.org/index.html

National Information Center for Children and Youth with Disabilities
www.nichcy.org

National Institute of Child Health and Human Development Clearinghouse
www.nichd.nih.gov

National Institute of Mental Health (NIMH)
www.nimh.nih.gov

National Organization for Rare Disorders (NORD)
www.rarediseases.org

Tourette Syndrome Association
www.tsa-usa.org

Publisher's Note:
The websites listed on this page were active at the time of publication. The publisher is not responsible for websites that have changed their address or discontinued operation since the date of publication. The publisher will review and update the websites upon each reprint.

Index

alpha-agonists 66, 76
amphetamine 68, 81
anticonvulsants 80
antidepressants 52, 65, 68
antihistamines 47
antihypertensives 68
antipsychotic drugs 45, 51, 82
anxiety (disorders) 7, 43, 51–52, 64
attention-deficit and disruptive behavior disorders (ADD) 12–13, 69, 80, 84, 117–119
attention-deficit/hyperactivity disorder (ADHD) 7–8, 29–32, 35, 42, 52, 67–68, 80–82, 84, 86, 89–92, 111, 114–119, 121
atypical antipsychotics 52, 61, 66, 69, 76, 80, 82
autism 20–27, 41, 51–52, 55, 66, 77–78, 85, 108–110, 112, 115

behavior therapy 83
benzodiazepines 52, 55, 76, 80
bipolar disorder 7, 55
brain 39, 47, 51–56, 60–67, 78, 81, 116

central nervous system (CNS) 51, 61–63, 65, 67, 115
chromosomes 39–42
communication disorders 12
coprolalia 17
copropraxia 17

depression 51–52, 55, 64, 66, 101, 118
Diagnostic and Statistical Manual for Mental Disorders, fourth edition (DSM-IV) 12, 16–17, 24, 31
diet 15, 108–109, 119
dopamine 51, 61, 64, 66–69, 75, 80

dopamine receptors 51, 66
Down syndrome 40–41, 105
drug approval 54
Drug Enforcement Administration 115
drug holidays 84
dyskinesias 52, 75, 100
dyslexia 18

echolalia 17, 94
echopraxia 17
elimination disorders 12

feeding and eating disorders of infancy or early childhood 12
fetal alcohol syndrome 42
Food and Drug Administration (FDA) 9, 50, 54, 76, 78–80

gamma-aminobutyric acid (GABA) 51, 112
genetic research 55
Gilles de la Tourette, Georges 58

Health Canada 54
Health Care Financing Administration (HCFA) 83
homeopathy 111
hyperactivity 7, 29–31, 34–35, 42, 52, 78, 119

inattention 31, 33–35, 84
intellectual disabilities 37–39, 83
impulsivity 31, 34–35, 66–67

learning disorders 12, 41
lithium 80

magnetic resonance imaging (MRI) 54

methylphenidate hydrochloride (Ritalin) 49, 52, 67, 80–81, 111, 115–116, 118
motor skills disorders 12

neurons 51, 61–65, 67–68
neuroleptics 69, 82, 100
neurotransmitters 51, 61, 64–65, 69, 81
noradrenergic reuptake inhibitors 81
norepinephrine 64, 68, 81

obsessive-compulsive disorder 18, 55
opiate receptor antagonists 82
opioid blockers 82

palilalia 17
panic disorder 55, 64
pervasive developmental disorders (PDD) 12–13, 22, 66, 70
Asperger's disorder 22
childhood disintegrative disorder 22
pervasive developmental disorder not otherwise specified 22, 24
Rett's disorder 22
psychotherapy 64, 69, 71, 83, 121

serotonin 51–52, 65–66, 68, 80, 83
selective serotonin reuptake inhibitors (SSRIs) 52, 65–66, 80, 102
schizophrenia 50–51, 55
single-photon emission computed tomography (SPECT) 54
stereotypy 69
stimulants 52, 65, 67–68, 92, 105, 115

tardive dyskinesia 75, 100
tension 16–17, 70, 76
tic disorders 12–13, 16–17, 52, 66
    chronic motor or vocal tic disorder 17
    tic disorder not otherwise specified 18
Tourette's syndrome 16
Transient tic disorder 17
tricyclic antidepressants (TCAs) 52, 65–66, 82
trisomy 40

vitamins (supplements) 109–110, 112, 121

About the Author & Consultants

Shirley Brinkerhoff was a writer, editor, speaker, and musician. She published six young adult novels, six informational books for young people, scores of short stories and articles, and taught at writers' conferences throughout the United States.

Mary Ann McDonnell, Ph.D., R.N., is the owner of South Shore Psychiatric Services, where she provides psychiatric services to children and adolescents. She has worked as a psychiatric nurse at Franciscan Hospital for Children and has been a clinical instructor for Northeastern University and Boston College advanced-practice nursing students. She was also the director of clinical trials in the pediatric psychopharmacology research unit at Massachusetts General Hospital. Her areas of expertise are bipolar disorder in children and adolescents, ADHD, and depression.

Donald Esherick has worked in regulatory affairs at Rhone-Poulenc Rorer, Wyeth Pharmaceuticals, Pfizer, and Pharmalink Consulting. He specializes in the chemistry section (manufacture and testing) of investigational and marketed drugs.

BAS 616.89 St291c

Childhood & adolescent disorders /

ELIZABETH